The Birds in Langfoot's Belfry

Studies in German Literature, Linguistics and Culture:
Translations from German Literature

Publisher's Note

The Birds in Langfoot's Belfry was translated from the original German text *Die Vögel des Herrn Langfoot* by Professor Elena B. Odio, who teaches language and literature at Georgia Southwestern College in Americus. The introduction was provided by Professor Ward B. Lewis, German Department of the University of Georgia.

This is the first English translation of the novel by Paul Zech (1881-1946), who is perhaps best known not for his prose works but for his expressionistic poetry, especially those poems that appeared in Kurt Pinthus's epoch-making anthology, *Menschheitsdämmerung* (1920; a translation by J. Ratych, R. Ley, and R. Conard appeared in this Camden House translation series in 1993). The novel arose when Zech was in exile in South America, having fled the Nazi regime in 1933. The book provides a unique picture of a sophisticated European living a kind of picaresque life in a culture for which he is ill prepared and which he ill understands. The exoticism of the rural scene stands in an interesting contrast to the whimsical flights of the cultured German. There is, reading between the lines, much of the Zeitgeist of the 1930s in this humorous, yet thought-provoking novel.

Paul Zech

The Birds in Langfoot's Belfry

Translated by Elena B. Odio
with a foreword by Ward B. Lewis

CAMDEN HOUSE

Translation copyright © 1994 by
CAMDEN HOUSE, INC.

Authorized translation licensed by the Greifenverlag zu Rudolstadt,
Germany.

Published by Camden House, Inc.
Drawer 2025
Columbia, SC 29202 USA

Printed on acid-free paper.
Binding materials are chosen for strength and
durability.

All Rights Reserved
Printed in the United States of America
First Edition

ISBN:1-57113-007-1

Library of Congress Cataloging-in-Publication Data

Zech, Paul, 1881-1946
 [Vögel des Herrn Langfoot. English]
 The birds in Langfoot's belfry / Paul Zech : translated by Elena B. Odio with a foreword by Ward B. Lewis. -- 1st ed.
   p.   cm. -- (Studies in German literature, linguistics, and culture)
 Includes bibliographical references.
 ISBN 1-57113-007-1 (alk. paper)
 I. Title. II. Series: Studies in German literature, linguistics, and culture (unnumbered)
 PT2653.E2V6413   1994
 833--dc20   94-1310
                                                             CIP

Table of Contents

Foreword   ix

The Birds in Langfoot's Belfry   1

Glossary   98

Translator's Note   103

Foreword

Paul Zech has been recently characterized as one of the most many-sided and productive lyrical talents of this century; however he did not confine himself to verse. Writing expansively in all genres, he left behind a massive body of creative work, and this provides a semi-autobiographical record of his characteristic attitudes and a reflection of his life. The pastoral lyricism of his early poetry reveals vitalism and awe of nature, which he describes by the use of religious and Biblical imagery. Workers' Poetry recalls his early occupation in coal mines and steel mills of the Ruhr, Belgium, and northern France. His inclinations towards the working class and politics on the left are revealed in novelle which depict economic exploitation and contain considerable criticism of capitalism. Military service in the First World War that left him seriously injured finds voice in pacifistic sentiments. He revered the great German poet Rainer Maria Rilke and the French poets Villon, Rimbaud, and Mallarmé among others whom he translated widely. Expressionism and New Objectivity are recognized in his style, which was eclectic throughout his lifetime and richly varied.

The author was incredibly prolific. More than two dozen anthologies of his poetry appeared, and he contributed innumerable poems to periodicals and journals. He wrote more than thirty dramas and a hundred prose works as well as literary critical studies, translations, and adaptations.

Paul Zech was born in 1881 in Briesen near Thorn, West Prussia, in what is now Poland, the son of a schoolteacher. There he first attended school eventually resettling in Elberfeld, North Rhine-Westphalia, where he became closely acquainted with the expressionist poet Else Lasker-Schüler. Her influence drew him to Berlin, and there during the pre-war years he moved in various literary circles and co-edited a journal of some renown. Drafted in 1915, he was stationed on the western front in France. A year later he was injured by a grenade and gas poisoning which caused a heart condition he bore the rest of his life.

Zech achieved the height of his fame during the decade after 1918, the year he received the prestigious Kleist Prize from Heinrich Mann. In 1920 he was recognized as a major voice of expressionism when twelve of his poems were chosen by Kurt Pinthus for inclusion in the anthology

Menschheitsdämmerung, the work that effectively identified the poets thereafter associated with this literary style. Six years later his version of Rimbaud's drama *Das trunkene Schiff* premiered in Berlin at the Volksbühne directed by Erwin Piscator with scenery by George Grosz.

The Third Reich ensured that exile should become Zech's fate and the subject of his late writing. In April 1933 he was arrested and held briefly; four months later he fled into exile leaving behind a wife and two children. By December he eventually found haven in Buenos Aires, where he joined his brother. Although Zech followed the course of the war and his thoughts dwelt upon Germany, he would never see his country again. In September 1946 he suffered a fatal stroke.

During the exile years Zech published only four works, including poetry, some tales, and a tribute to his good friend in exile, the author Stefan Zweig. These were published in Buenos Aires. He continued to write during this time, however, and created a great corpus of completed material. To date only a segment of this work has appeared posthumously.

A number of publishers supported him at various stages in his career. In 1924 the Greifenverlag in Rudolstadt, Thuringia brought out both a collection of his poetry and a volume of short, autobiographical sketches; after his death this firm remained the predominant publisher of his literary estate. The typescript of *Die Vögel des Herrn Langfoot* is held by the Academy of Arts in Berlin, where the date 1939 is to be seen opposite the flyleaf. It is this text which appeared in a shortened version from the Greifenverlag in 1954.

The works written during the exile period allow themselves to be brought together into three groups. The largest of these consists of collections of Indian tales and legends; intended to appeal to German reading tastes for exotic travel literature, they were purportedly of Indian derivation but probably conceived by Zech. Other writing includes stories dealing with German immigrants and their struggles to survive and adapt; here the author details the racist attitudes of Creoles and newcomers, especially regarding Indians. A third group of works are those novels dealing with the theme of exile and are stridently anti-fascist in tone.

Although *The Birds in Langfoot's Belfry* treats the life of a German immigrant, who is also an exile figure, this short novel distinguishes itself from Zech's other writing in that it offers adventure, social criticism, satire, and a touch of the picaresque.

While in exile Zech himself never felt comfortable in his new environment; the author was depressed, homesick, and despondent; he did not fit in. Langfoot, on the other hand, while every bit as self-conscious as the author in exile, can be energetic, happy-go-lucky, and optimistic.

And further comparisons are justified. Zech subtitled the work 'a not untrue story,' and the reflection of the author in his fictional central figure is distinct. Zech claimed to have studied at Heidelberg and affected the academic title 'Doctor' when reviewing his own anonymous poems in German journals. Just as Zech, Johann Peter Langfoot, Ph.D., Heidelberg reaches Buenos Aires in flight from a Europe facing spiritual and moral dissolution. Langfoot is a literary figure from Berlin, who attempts unsuccessfully to found an exile journal in his host country. Since this *gringo* offers an easy prey to the crafty Argentines, he gravitates towards the immigrant community. Although those about him tout the supposed economic and political advantages to be gained by another war, he as the bearer of an injury acquired during trench warfare in World War I knows better.

'Timm' was the pseudonym that Zech had adopted while still in Berlin to conceal the authorship of writing left in its political orientation; it is a name which he maintained in exile to cloak his antifascist activity. Langfoot is accompanied by his comrade Timm when he leaves Buenos Aires behind him, and what they see appears through Zech's political eyes: for example, a camp of exploited immigrant laborers and the grossly unequal distribution of property – evidence of a dominant class that makes the laws and controls the police. The operation of the economic system forces social outsiders to develop their own support system.

In another work completed probably less than a year earlier Langfoot also appears, and here he bears an even closer resemblance to Zech or at least to the image he conceived of himself. In *Deutschland, dein Tänzer ist der Tod* (1980) Langfoot is the author of a pacifistic drama and member of the anti-Nazi resistance. He must flee into exile to Buenos Aires, where three months after arrival he meets an acquaintance with whom he was earlier associated in productions of the Volksbühne in Berlin. In conversation Langfoot expresses Zech's attitudes towards exile and exile authors and especially his resentment towards the predominant influence of brown politics among the German immigrant colony.

The central figure in the work before us is a good-humored fellow, who resents being taken for granted by others. He has considerable pride in himself as a German and, vis-à-vis the Indians, as a Caucasian. He has a well-developed social conscience regarding the division of goods and property. Langfoot is independent and thinks that what becomes of him will be the consequence of his own actions and of fate. This last force is represented by the birds in his head, which he credits with providing him the freedom to commit himself to unpremeditated action. Sometimes decisions can be left to them, as, for example, whether to prepare himself for work as a teacher among the German colony at Terrabussa.

With a deft touch Elena Odio captures the multitude of meanings behind the German idiom 'to have a bird (in one's head).' This figure of speech may be a reference to an obsession and is translated by one dictionary as 'having a bee in one's bonnet'; but such renderings are not entirely appropriate in Langfoot's case. Keeping close to the literal meaning of the German, Odio alludes to 'feathered friends' or 'larks' occupying Langfoot's skull, playing off against the additional connotation for the latter term of 'whims' or 'fancies.' For indeed, Langfoot is capricious.

His carefree, uninhibited, irreverent behavior brings to mind Till Eulenspiegel, a popular jester from the fourteenth century, the collected anecdotes of whom illustrate the cunning with which he holds his own against society. And Langfoot compares himself to Ahasuerus, the Wandering Jew, as well as Peter Schlemihl, the nineteenth-century Romantic character doomed to search for his shadow.

But Langfoot's roots as a literary figure lie in the tradition of the picaresque novel and its first important German representative, the collection concerning the *picaro* Simplicissimus. Originating in sixteenth century Spain this genre comprises the prose autobiography of a rogue hero, who describes his adventures in a satire of the society he exploits. A century later Simplicissimus appeared as the central figure of H. J. Grimmelshausen's novel, which as the work before us is loose and episodic in structure as well as realistic, socially critical, and satirical.

Arriving as he does from Europe, Langfoot is a *gringo* who can never achieve status among Argentineans. He is a displaced person, peripatetic and destitute, living by his wits. Langfoot begins as a small-time confidence man. Inspired by sexual fantasies of pleasures no longer enjoyed by the husband of his Madonna and granted the insight that he must have status, or the appearance of it, to achieve success, Langfoot models his strategy after that of the sexual athlete Vandotti.

The vagabond lives by his resourcefulness sizing up a ranch, access thereto, and its occupants. With a cock-and-bull story he explains his background, and the prospect of an inheritance fuels his calculating schemes.

That aching knee which he bears as a memento from the war tells him to keep moving, and indeed he does, on a circular path along the edge of society until eventually reaching Buenos Aires again. Adopted by the Langmanns and moved forward, he achieves a degree of integration among the immigrants and their children that they themselves have not yet reached in Argentine society.

There is the suggestion that Langfoot becomes domesticated, that those ingrained vagabond ways that he emphasized to Paulina and exercised in flight from her and others have been reformed. Another young, unmarried heiress appears as the thirteen-year-old Marie-Louise. And the fact that he asks himself whether his petit bourgeois status constitutes a pause in his career or the end of it and, characteristically, that he will discuss the question with Timm suggests its own answer.

Zech worked at his writing and rewrote until the day he died. Chapter Thirteen of *Die Vögel des Herrn Langfoot* reflects a version of the tale very close to the unpublished original and not entirely consistent with the rest of the work in regard to the image it projects of the central figure. In this chapter the *picaro* Langfoot meets his match.

After two years Langfoot returns to Buenos Aires via the Paraná river from Paraguay, having parted company with smugglers under favorable financial circumstances. The chapter that follows constitutes a flashback and provides the first indication that we have not been considering Langfoot's history in a chronological fashion since his first arrival in this foreign country. A time is recalled in the life of Langfoot with which the reader has not become familiar in the course of the work. Indeed, a Langfoot is introduced who is an entire dimension removed from that street person who lit out from Buenos Aires for the provinces. It is as if Zech forgot that he had not shown us our hero exercising his secretarial skills in French and German for an export firm at a comfortable salary of one hundred and eighty pesos a month; he is the purchaser of men's wear and frequenter of the opera.

The exile Langfoot assumes a sentimental familiarity with countrymen, often on short acquaintance, that allows him to be played for a sucker. Our hero becomes open handedly generous and permits himself to be shamefully exploited. That lengthy odyssey that took Langfoot from the capital across the countryside to Paraguay and back is reflected on a smaller scale by the eight-week trip undertaken with Zumbusch when they leave town to work in the fields. The conclusion is, however, this time less fortunate. The gift of the silver stickpin to Rosita upon the eve of Langfoot's departure, and the associations he makes with it while narrating in retrospect, provide a presentiment of what will occur. Three weeks before Langfoot's return Rosita will have married Zumbusch.

The archives of the Academy of Arts hold a typescript of Chapter Fifteen of the work that never saw print. This amounts to ninety-two pages omitted from the final, shortened, published version. Just as Langfoot, the *picaro*, is outwitted by his countryman Zumbusch so the poor fellow here too falls easy prey, this time to a German exile couple. The independence, self-reliance, and confidence that Langfoot displays in the published work is nowhere evident here. The humorous story is told of Langfoot's involvement with Lütti, ostensible professor of philosophy, and his bleached blond wife, the fastidious Frau Lusam, née Pflaumenmus (plum jam). In writing which is very much oriented towards the politics of exile, description is provided of how the couple reached Buenos Aires from Paris; there in immigrant circles they had hobnobbed with Leopold Schwarzschild, editor of the journal *Das Tage-Buch*, and the renowned actress Elisabeth Bergner – both of whom would eventually find refuge in the United States.

Recollections of Germany move Langfoot as well as sympathy for countrymen sharing an exile fate. The three join forces as the so-called Trinity Community to rent a chalet, where the professor will live according to what he takes to be the fashion of Goethe and devote himself to a book on Einstein. As the sole source of income Langfoot is saddled with all expenses and bears them without objection, acquiescing phlegmatically with little apparent awareness of how he is being exploited.

It is Timm Borah to the rescue. Denouncing Lusam as a Nazi and her husband as a charlatan, Timm influences Langfoot's decision to break with them on grounds that are clearly political. But Borah doesn't trust to his friend's steadfastness and assumes the initiative, providing when he moves out transportation for his belongings and accommodations.

Zech himself was never politically active. In 1918 he undertook propaganda for the socialist German republic, but he didn't see himself as a member of the working class. He endorsed the short-lived Popular Front; and it has been observed that since he supported the communist resistance to Hitler, Zech's politics during exile had moved to the left. I suggest, however, that he remained equivocatingly moderate.

It is a fallacy, of course, to attribute words of a character to the beliefs of the author. Langfoot speaks, however, curiously like Zech. The character dissolves his association with the Trinity Community because he waits confidently for world revolution – if not during these war years, then shortly thereafter. And in a tavern frequented by Germans the conversation turns to the subject of revolution and the seizure of power. In the text – here omitted – of the typescript the lines of Langfoot's remarks are heavily reworked in the author's hand, suggesting that Zech sought carefully to express himself clearly. Here before his beer drinking countrymen Langfoot calls for prudent individual consideration of the path and goals of revolution; he warns that confused 'ultra-proletarian raving' may impede progress.

A word regarding structure and style. Appearing first in the title, the dominant image of the shorter published novel is reflected in aspects of its construction. The effect of those birds which flutter and swoop to precipitate excitement, distraction, and confusion is sometimes manifested in the pattern of text. This may be disjointed in the dialogue of characters, erratic in its sequence, and often flippant in a manner verging on pedantry. The thoughts of the narrator occasionally skip from one association to another in an abrupt and disconnected fashion.

The voice of the narrator is rich in inflections, bitter, and almost sardonic when detailing Langfoot's status as a *gringo*. Irony finds expression regarding poverty: "... this outrageous disparity between debit and credit ... was the daily routine, and the charming prospect existed that the situation would never improve."

The narrator plays with the reader as, for example in Chapter Six, where the objective voice provides a description of the weary Langfoot falling asleep in the tool shed of Vandotti. Omniscience enables the speaker to relate that Langfoot dreams; but distance is eliminated and the reader acknowledged and at the same time abandoned to curiosity by the utterance "Not one smidgen of Langfoot's dream is to be aired here." The reader reconciles himself to unfulfilled expectations only to learn just lines later that Langfoot's Madonna was the subject of his subconscious.

When Zech employs associations or connections that are so fantastic that the meaning is lost, his technique outstrips the reader. For that reason the original version of 1954 annotated linguistic items for the author's German readership. In Chapter Four Timm alludes to the successful medical practice of his cousin, whose office is complete with "chocolate-coated pastries imported from Brazil," thus Odio's rendering of "Paulistaner Mohrenköpfe," the latter term meaning literally 'Moors' Heads' and referring to a well-known chocolate delight; the proper adjective is derived from Paul. So where does that leave us? Only in the light of the annotation from 1954 might the reader surmise that Zech is here alluding to blacks from the city of São Paulo in Brazil.

The metaphoric language of the novel illustrates the close interrelationship between nature and man, between plant and animal. A man's grizzled temples are compared, for example, with the torn bark of the eucalyptus trees. Tree roots are like the skin of an ancient turtle. An underground stream in its flow is compared with the sap from a broken flower stalk as it drips and hardens into stonelike drops. Air is described as too fragile to allow the cicadas to spin out the glistening thread of their melody to its conclusion. Zech provides a vivid picture of the savanna fire in Chapter Seven, a dynamic event wherein Langfoot witnesses the convulsions and devastation followed by a storm.

Odio conveys a feeling for the German which shimmers behind her translation. This is particularly true when idioms are rendered in such a way as to convey their meaning and yet retain a quality that distinguishes them in English. In Chapter Ten Langfoot leaves the employ of Eric Laase at the lumber mill, by whom he had been treated shabbily. In the German

Langfoot expresses his relief at leaving the place behind with a reference to crossing himself three times. The idiomatic expression 'to make three crosses after something or someone' has a history of its own in the language; according to the brothers Grimm it originated with a practice undertaken as protection against the unpleasant reoccurrence of a person, event, or experience.

The German edition of 1954 provided a glossary which has been substantially reworked for the sake of accuracy, supplementation, and the elimination of Spanish terms generally known to a North American reading audience. Literary references are included as well as more obscure geographical allusions.

The Mystery of Chapter Fifteen

It came to my attention that the contents of Chapter Fifteen in the typescript held by the Archive of the Academy of Arts, Berlin has been omitted completely from the published novel. This typescript includes handwritten corrections and changes made by the author.

On a leaf following the title page Zech designates above his signature this typescript as copy number one. He purports to reserve the rights to translation, presentation, radio, and film with the line "Coyright [sic] 1939 by Dr. Paul Zech / Buenos Aires / Argentina." I will refer to this typescript as A.

An analysis of Chapter Fifteen indicates something of its history. The pages in DIN A4 are hand numbered in the lower, right-hand corner continuously from 231 through 351, with page 232 missing.

The chapter is divided into eight sections with a roman numeral in the upper, left-hand corner between 2 to 3 1/2 c.m. from the edge of the paper. An exception is posed by section III, which will be considered below.

The first line of the first paragraph in each section is indented; otherwise there is no indentation. Sections I and VII present some inconsistent internal indentation.

Each section concludes above three asterisks in the center of the page which function as a marker. In section I this role is performed by the proper name "Lusam" written in upper case.

Each section begins on a page of its own, the single exception to this practice appearing on page 344 where VII concludes above the asterisks and VIII commences below.

Sometime after the conclusion of A in 1939 and before his death in 1946 Zech undertook extensive revisions. I refer to these as B. He employed a different typewriter than that used for A, a fact readily distinguishable upon inspection of the fonts for the letter "a" – both lower and upper case. In A the upper case font is very narrow and the bowl of the lower case font horizontal; in B these are wide and round, respectively. Although both typewriters had the umlaut, they both lacked the character "ß."

The changes introduced as B reduced the original 121 pages to 90, and those pages removed are no longer extant. The pages of B were inserted in various places, and these are unnumbered.

Whereas in the published version of the novel the chapters receive a number at the top of the first page of text and this reference stands alone, in the typescript of B Chapter Fifteen has its own title page and receives a subtitle, namely "<u>Das fünfzehnte Kapitel</u> oder die Dreieinige Gemeinsamkeit Luhsam, Lütti und Co."

Zech concerned himself for the most part with the conclusions of the various sections. The last four pages of I became one page. The twenty-five pages from 267 through 292, including the conclusion of II and III in its entirety, was reduced to eleven pages in II and four in III. The latter constituted the entire section, and no roman numeral was assigned although the first line of the first paragraph was indented. Similarly, the last two pages in IV were reduced to one page and the last two of VI to one. Internally both pages 235-36 and 244-45 were each reduced to one page. Pages 313-16 were removed and not replaced. The eleven pages from 321 through 331 were reduced to two.

The fact that Zech designated this typescript as the first copy suggests that he may have reproduced it for acquaintances as was his wont. I have been unable to locate any others; it is reasonable, therefore, to assume that the first copy was considered for publication. After Zech's death and before the posthumous appearance of the book in 1954, the decision was made to omit Chapter Fifteen of the typescript in its entirety. This was probably done by the editors at Greifenverlag, who have provided no confirmation of this point. One can only speculate regarding the reasons for excluding the material.

The editors may have decided to omit the chapter because of its disproportionate size; its various sections are comparable in length to the individual chapters published. The inclusion of this material would have shifted the focus of the work from the adventures of a picaresque hero to an insider's view of his countrymen in exile. Such a change of emphasis would not have enhanced the novel. The subject of exile did not excite the popular imagination in 1954, less than a decade after the demise of the Third Reich. Indeed, asylum in exile seemed faintly treasonous, and Germanists had yet to discover the field of exile literature and make it respectable. By 1980, however, when Zech's work *Deutschland, dein Tänzer ist der Tod* appeared, all that had changed.

In the typescript Zech fails to keep his material at arm's length; he is very involved personally and politically with his subject. The author names names, and characters are identifiable as well as places such as restaurants, for example, which they frequent. The figures in exile appear in an unfavorable light as if inhabiting an underworld; and Greifenverlag may well have wished to avoid the risk of defamation. For example, the narrator describes a pathetic and miserable figure known in Paris from 1933 to 1936, who fed and clothed himself with scraps. Reference is made to the kraal bursting with comrades in suffering, where he dwelt, and the horrible stench. This figure is given the name "Dr. Anselmo" and described as the editor of the writings of the political philosopher Max Stirner. The person behind this character is most certainly Anselm Ruest, who edited works by Stirner, contributed to German language exile newspapers in Paris, and died in 1943 in exile in France. That Zech does not hesitate to make such identifications, indeed that he actually relishes name dropping, is evident upon examination of the typescript, where references are sharpened to remove ambiguity. We read, for example, that the swindler Lütti had dined at the home of Hugo Simon and wore his suits; before the name of Hugo Simon, Zech inserts in handwriting 'the former Berlin banker.'

Chapter Fifteen was important to Zech, and he devoted great attention to it. The writing provided a psychological outlet of a particular nature. Throughout his professional life Zech saw himself in keen competition with others for public recognition and felt that he failed to receive his due. Uneasiness and jealousy provoked outbursts and generated personal and literary feuds. In Chapter Fifteen, as elsewhere in his literary estate, Zech employs gossip and innuendo to denigrate writers or political figures, settling scores as he repays rivals for slights imagined and real.

Ward B. Lewis

Chapter One

Neither the city nor even the territory surrounding the River Plate had witnessed the birth of Johann Peter Langfoot. He had come uninvited to Buenos Aires and had brought with him heavy intellectual baggage from that section of Europe which in his opinion was undergoing complete moral and intellectual disintegration.

The tall palm trees around the port area were, in their own way, trying to soothe the anxieties that Johann Peter still carried within him. They bore proud testimony to their tropical origins, even though the freezing rain had left them quite disheveled. Behind this gigantic broomlike awning which, despite its proportions, could not sweep away the trashy black clouds overhead, the not altogether pleasing silhouette of Buenos Aires made itself visible. This was the city that had bestowed on him the *gringo* label so customary in those parts but with which he was at a total loss. Come early morning he would give anything for a pile of wood to saw and split in some darkened farmyard. Or let him have a rug to beat, marble steps to sweep, and a wooden floor to polish. Or again, the wonderful sensation of biting into a fat loaf of bread; but he was too ashamed to beg for it. He spotted a tasty looking roll of bread sitting on a window sill on upper Talcahuana Street. But before he could make up his mind to take it, he had to walk past the window sill three times in carefully measured steps as if waiting for a pretty girl. Then he looked for the shadiest park bench he could find close by and ate. With time he developed a routine for collecting leftover bread. But that was not enough to put his hunger to rest. At last, after three months, he was accepted into a gang of drifters. For it had finally dawned on him that to cop scraps successfully you must first take some lessons. In chronological terms he was already much too old to be any sort of quick learner. Average was as good as he got. He had to make exceptionally wide turns around a great number of things to avoid stepping on any toes. For if he had exceeded the limits set for him, he would have remained indefinitely a *gringo* to be merely tolerated. Personally, of course, he wished to be rid of the entire designation in the quickest possible way. But for him, who had already been around the entire European continent, half of Asia, and a good part of Africa, it was no longer possible to extricate himself from that mask without outside help. It meshed with his true features. He wasn't even startled when the large mirror windows of the fashionable cafés put him face to face with it at night. He posted himself at the curb where the cars would drive up and opened and closed their doors. There were evenings when he might collect sixty *centavos* in tips this way, but on average they came only to fifty. And because he was no worse at this job than the local experts, he was eventually entrusted with a box of collar buttons. His appointed strip was a narrow side street by the *Constitución* train station. And with that he had reached the nethermost rung in the local business establishment. By the time his fourth week on the job had rolled around, he pondered whether it might not be time to send off a detailed report to his relatives in Europe, along with promises of a money order in solid *pesos*. For the time being, however, he was unable to carry out this good intention because postage alone would have swallowed up half a day's income. To him, this outrageous disparity between debit and credit was a very thorny issue, especially since he had never before experienced it in such violent terms. Here it was the daily routine, and the charming prospect existed that the situation would never improve.

However, after seven more weeks there was some improvement. From shirt buttons he moved up to peppermint rolls and from lozenges on to a bundle of lottery tickets. In subsequent weeks he went around the local bars with razor blades. He was doing business, but he was not paying government licensing fees. There were, scattered about the entire city, countless such establishments ideally suited for the illegal sale of smuggled merchandise. The same smell could also be found swirling everywhere. It was an oil spiced by earthen juices; in it fish were roasted, pastries were baked, and *ñandú* eggs were allowed to run golden. Nestled between these over *quebracho* wood coals on the iron grill lay crackling the suet of lambs, calves, and armadillos, and of piglets as tender as marzipan. And amidst it all blared the scratchy radios, all similarly attuned – dispensing cultural caviar from the ether for the population at large. Music for complacent personalities, designed to improve and quicken the digestion.

After another five weeks he dropped the razor blade line. His net worth stood at 23.50 *pesos*. Out of that, for a shoeshine stand and paraphernalia that stood on the *Plaza Once* he paid a man fifteen *pesos*.

Autumn finally decided it had postponed its arrival long enough; it made its entrance official with a heavy rainstorm. And in seal weather like that hardly anyone wanted to have his shoes polished. The city looked on with an unusual grouchy-dumb expression. Doors opening into establishments were now actually doors again, and not just strings hanging there fringelike, or mere flour sacks. The smell of grilled meat reached the street only by intervals now, and it didn't care one whit about the growling stomach of a shoeblack who'd been sold the worst stand of them all. The blood went to Langfoot's head whenever someone rushed by who hadn't seen a brush on his shoes in the last three days. He attributed the flushed look of the passersby to the weather. And from the weather his thoughts again turned to the city. He had long since put the mismatched dwellings out of his mind; it no longer occurred to him to see the fractured skyline as an aggravation. Matters of that sort, with thousands of permutations, were a daily routine here; so why immediately shed tears over them? Nor was he upset any more by the endlessly long streets. He lived at their outermost limit, at a point where the numbering reached 7000 and above. He and six others were living in that barnlike hole. And of them only he, Johann Peter Langfoot, who held a doctoral degree from Heidelberg University, was the *gringo*; he hadn't shaken that label yet.

A *gringo*, that's what he was, even for the people who returned to his shoeshine stand time after time because Johann Peter knew his trade. He was just one out of a vast number of foreigners: a German with the name Johann Peter Langfoot. With time he might have forgotten even that, but coincidentally it was stated in his travel documents which, as it happened, were now reduced to a single fragment of paper bearing official seals.

Chapter Two

Who could shed tears over a business that brought in just enough *pesetas* to barely cover the cost of a hole in which to sleep and a choice of either pea or noodle broth down at the soup kitchen?!

Johann Peter Langfoot was certainly none the sadder to see himself fall back into unemployment because of a 'lack of business sense.' He wished to remain honest while doing business, and that was not considered proper in a country about whose governing class the word was that it ceased to steal only when a certain windpipe ceased to function. But he ran across a good-natured Swabian who gave him the splendid piece of advice − enhanced by a ten-*peso* bill − that he should leave the overcrowded federal capital and visit some of the underpopulated inland settlements. This was no April Fool's joke, in his opinion, and that advice together with the promise of better weather conditions led him to hang around such establishments as would undertake that type of city-country exchange for a reasonable fee. He found people there who, like himself, were willing to try and extract new delights from Tierra del Fuego or the

Gran Chaco. Now whether there is, in fact, any substantial difference between the city and the provinces from the standpoint of the individual intent on making his life more bearable, that issue none of his traveling companions could be sure of; there were no three or seven year warranties to be had. After years of riding the rails for free, these men had acquired a time-tested routine. They were born *lyngheras*, or tramps you might say, and their hemp travel sacks and cooking utensils had been ready for weeks.

As the years go by the city eventually becomes too confining for everybody. To compensate, people go out in search of the sea or the mountains. They run around out in the country as fishermen or farmers and approximate their lifestyle to that of the livestock. Excepting, of course, that they disdain grass and would not, for any amount of money, dispense with their seven course noon meal. On the other hand, when such a man sees how happily the livestock lives out its existence in the bright sunshine, that attitude seems to him a healthy and happy one. His only problem is that he has found nowhere among the natives a companion able to seduce him and with whom to indulge in the God given joys of nature. Notwithstanding all of that, he still bathes naked in the reed pond and regularly comes down with the sniffles as a result. The upshot of it all is that after a while the country and its bucolic charms seem absolutely insufferable to him. Besides, the opera season has already begun and a new series of sound movies starring Marlene Dietrich is underway.

All of these people are of the opinion that an educated individual can only lead the cultured lifestyle that he deserves if he lives in the capital. In return they are more than willing to contribute whatever it takes at the stock market and in the export-import offices. One does what one can, even calling on one's wits occasionally. The resources upon which the brain will draw, however, are of no concern at all to the participants. People behave here as with vintage wines: the more dust and calcium deposits a bottle displays, the more the dummies have to shell out for it, and one never runs out of the gullible ones, as we know.

No wonder then, that Johann Peter Langfoot also quickly insisted on finding the city horrible. Every street looks like the next one, and every house looks like its neighbor although the external dimensions can be very different; similarly, both the *tranvía* and the *colectivo* are basically means of transportation from one terminal to another, not to mention those automobiles one sees studded with silver, ivory, and mother of pearl (whose latest models even come equipped with flushing toilets and television). But a freight train that spends twenty, thirty hours rattling across the endless expanses of the landscape past grazing cattle, fields of wheat, tobacco plantations, and palm groves on its way to the Andean plateau, well ... that's an entirely different matter.

It occurred to Johann Peter Langfoot that to head off into the wild blue yonder with a group was something that could just as well be arranged *mañana*. I still lack a couple of deep breaths of city before I can break this addiction of mine, he thought. There is certainly not one of these streets down which I haven't walked in my everlasting condition of grimy poverty. And yet I am merely a marginal inhabitant of this city. Just a common outsider. Truly a *gringo*. This non-existence as an unsteady individual who has never met with success anywhere might just as well be tailored to my profile – like a mannequin on which an entire segment of the population could be tailored. People who are counted but who don't tip the scales; people who are made note of, but who don't figure in. The same people who, because no one admits their opinion, are prevented from ever even reaching a position with a pension fund. The same ones who relax in the sun because they've finally come to the realization that relaxation is in itself human and should not be allowed to atrophy; the same people often seen leaning back and savoring the rain because it is no more watery than the blood they can still occasionally wring from bad business deals and from the daily kicks administered by a city they weren't born into. And with it all one is supposed to do abeyance to its ordinances (themselves anything but orderly), whiff the aroma of money only from a good distance, and not frighten peace-loving citizens with a face in which the wind itself is lucky to find a spot.

At the last minute Johann Peter Langfoot remembered to drop his sister a line congratulating her on her birthday. If the ship transporting the letter is in luck, it will probably make the trip in three weeks, and the letter will get there in time. He wrote her that he was about to set off on yet another research expedition to explore as yet unseen parts of the interior:

"I will be forced to expose myself to certain dangers. If I make it through, consider it to have been done in the interest of the human race. What projects are you involved with as these summer days draftily unwind where fat apples lie on the road to Kohlhaasenbrück and iridescent leaves fall from the maple trees? It's really charming of you folks to leave me at the mercy of charity and table scraps.

"Now in the real wilderness things actually proceed quite decently. Hence my upcoming trip there ... the only such trip I plan to make. My cooking utensil, however, isn't ready yet. I still have to go look for it. Meanwhile the uninhibited youth of the birds in my brain continues to chirp, '*muy bien*!' and '*mach's gut*, you son of a gun!' I figure you're able to reason out how that's meant, since we two have, on many a previous occasion, discussed my 'larks' in more candid terms than now.... In your last letter you called me a devious dog because I turned away from the beloved linden trees back on the Rhine in such an disrespectful way. You were wrong, my dear. Today, in fact, I hear only the coughing of fleas and feel homesick for the nightingale's wings. I must penetrate very deep into the past to remember that old love of mine. It hurts to have the sensation that beings once frozen into shrines will never breathe again. Do you hear, sis? Never! Now and forever it will be a love for the dead. I have long since woven the funeral wreath. There are more thorns than roses on it. Perhaps a bouquet of reseda as well; but whatever you do, for heaven's sake that's the one you mustn't yank out. And finally, you must also remember that you are not Deborah, but that you're called Elisabeth. This is the only way I wish to see you again. Wholly or not at all. In other words, complete with all of my birds...."

It was only to break with the habit that Johann Peter Langfoot took one last trip out to the fields at Flores. His bunkmate went with him. They sat down beneath a weather-beaten gray eucalyptus and looked for a long time at the watering holes out of which they had regularly scooped little, blue pygmy fish. The fog still hung smokelike over the prairie grass. The sun had only been up for two hours, but already it was radiating a fair amount of heat, an invigorating current of springlike air felt in the innermost parts of the lung. It is a pleasant feeling to lie on one's back and send travel-eager thoughts scurrying after the feathery white clouds above. The head does not even notice that the roots on which it is propped are still chilly fresh and matted like the skin of an ancient turtle. Amidst the tree's diminutive leaves, not a trace of even the slightest dewdrop was discernible. A plump cardinal sat cleaning his feathers on one of the lowest branches while it gently swayed. A very rare guest for a location frequented by so many people. He could well be the last of a breed that had resided here for many centuries. A refugee from the noisy city. A pretty bird with a voice, a dark tuxedo topped with a flaming red crest. A wild creature that has dumped its digestive offal on the city and managed to cover a lot of ground as a result ... of its own perspective on this particular city, of course. Johann Peter Langfoot really didn't want to think the cardinal story through to its conclusion. But because his buddy Timm gave him such a knowing sideways glance, all but saying, As if your head weren't already possessed of enough such fine feathered fowl ... ; but you may as well let that one in too, because one more or less is not going to change things, he had to accommodate him with some sort of answer, and therefore mainly for his own benefit he mumbled, "That bird certainly does make a difference, my friend, because it is a cardinal. A bird – and a cardinal. But let's drop the subject because philosophy, generally speaking, doesn't even bring in the five *centavos* it takes to buy a daily newspaper, no matter how basic the subject might be to our life here on earth. So why should man bother spending any time thinking if it takes him no further than where he was? On the contrary, people commonly say, 'Man is reentering the Neolithic Age ... ,' in a tone of voice that still has the hollow ring of the other voice they were listening to just a few moments ago on the radio, the one they took as seriously as St. Anthony once took the love songs of the little girls that were trying to seduce him."

Bueno, said Johann Peter Langfoot to himself, if getting the latest gazettes hinges on the five *centavos* that one doesn't have, then one will have to be content with a newspaper that is already ten days old and utterly faded out by the weather. And yet so much is still discernible between the lines that two rational individuals can read themselves full enough to later become nauseous.

Chapter Three

They read ten day-old newspapers until after noon.... Until the grasses had already begun to rustle and the lizard was no longer afraid to risk its serpentine head out of hiding and flash the yellow gleam of its eyes. "The smell of war is permeating the air again!" Langfoot remarked on returning the newspaper to his companion.

"What if it is?" Timm answered, "I only wish that something would make its way here smelling or tasting like war. When the smoke is billowing there, when the air stinks there, when fatherless children whimper and the young widows are in dire straits trying to find a new provider in a hurry.... That's when we're sure to find decent work hereabouts and be rewarded with gold *pesos*."

"Well ... Timm, my friend, I can't even remember what those jobs taste like where people get a weekly salary. If only there were at least an aftertaste left on the tongue so that a person could have a foretaste of the next one. As it is, we're reduced to a state of powerlessness and can't even be sure of cash advances."

"You'll soon find that appetizing enough. At least it's better than having your belly blown open by grenade shrapnel. Be patient. Very soon we'll be coming up on the cattle herds. Out among the herds we'll experience how beef and hide prices have a fresh lure. We'll also catch a few crumbs off the great profits out there. And if we keep a close eye on our coins, maybe the sun will hatch us a piece of land. And should the seasons be fruitful, we too will ultimately own a herd, become Abraham the chosen, and no longer remember that we were once called *gringos* here."

"You've been carrying that hogwash around in your head for twenty years now, Timm. But you'll need to keep percolating it for a good while yet. Or do you seriously think that a desk drawer full of plenty can be instantly produced out of a pile of nothing? I don't want to have anything to do with war; I don't care. That's one matter I pass on, because the trenches are something I left behind me a long time ago. I am opposed to any aperture that looks like the crater left by a shell. To me any profits that might be derived from this war aren't worth a song. Whether the benefits are political or economic makes no difference because both relate to one another like a matching suit of clothes. I can no longer pretend to ignore that I have not been able to change shirts in five weeks. I have no others to my name. So that if I were to go down to the creek right now and wash my shirt – the way the Prussians taught us to do – then only the services of a highly trained mathematician would be adequate for the individual pieces to be successfully reassembled.

"Nor do I understand why it must be me, of all people, who has to hang around these parts. Even though I have often pinpointed what I want, there are nothing but obstacles looking me straight in the face. Even my big toe has finally caught on to that. Shortly before death it haunts the last hole in my shoe, happy soon to be wandering in the realm of the eternal Shades."

"Off with the shoe! A big toe that is suddenly conveyed out into the fresh air needn't immediately turn into Vergil."

"But ... what if I really did ride the rails with you for a stretch; can you tell me with any accuracy where the journey would end and what the good man looks like whom God or the Devil chose to provide me with a meager living?

"Even the fact that no one shows up here and tries to keep me from stretching out full length whenever I feel so inclined ... , that too, is beginning to get a little boring."

"Yes indeed ... , o worthy colleague; one becomes seriously ill and inwardly insensitive. One is no longer startled at all by the life a certain mother's favorite child must lead in these latitudes. At times I even feel as if I were standing outside of everything that is taking place around me."

"I know exactly where you're coming from, nightingale; you're not just talkin'," Timm replied in dialect. "Between us things could be golden ... if only you just didn't have such a goddam unnatural fear of traveling, of course!"

"Who's afraid?"

"Who? I mean, the word has made it out far and wide that you are petrified, and I mean complete with trousers splitting at the seams," laughed Timm.

"Am I a kangaroo still stuck inside its mother's pouch that I must bear the leaping imposed on me by these times?"

"And so, my dearest Peterjahn, if in future you should not wish to be as organized as that Australian creature … , *bueno*! Then we must spring into action tonight and steer in that direction. As for the destination … , that should be the least of our worries. Let's get out of here — and feel some movement again!"

"And what of the war, my good friend Timm, what of the war?"

"Frankly, that specter is ten days old at this point. If we could afford a newspaper hot off the presses, you would notice that the war hasn't finished cooking, even now. Matter of fact, I think it still won't have come to a boil by the time we've put a distance of two thousand miles between ourselves and this cage full of monkeys."

Chapter Four

They pressed on for another few minutes into the meadows. From the grass there rose the smell of rotten garbage and cow dung. There was a shimmering haze in the distance. Palely the walls of the distant city seemed to crowd together. The odd, milky light of day took the sharp edge off everything. The smooth-surfaced trunks of the trees reflected the sky's most vivid colors, playing unnatural tricks … on the observers' five senses. Amateur photographers were never able to capture this flickering sort of panorama, and they would ascribe their failure, albeit reluctantly, to deeper reasons. For example, to the whiff or whim of cosmic rays….

But there were painters who were at home with every aspect of this land. They portrayed it in a mad spectrum of colors. They produced trees that were blue, rust-red, ocher, and deep purple. They built walls of scarlet and orange, gold and amber, adding a meadow with the dull shimmer of peacock-blue satin velvet with human faces in it that were ivory and pale olive green.

These people saw a landscape just the way natural reality had shaped it. And in their paintings one saw a very close rendition. However, the spectators were few in number who gave any importance to the pictures and their creators. These were referred to as 'madmen.' This was the theme that ran — doubtless not without purpose — through the thoughts of Johann Peter Langfoot.

A single set of train tracks sliced the expanse in two. Through the crumpled weeds, a ditch full of nearly motionless water drew several diagonal lines. Here the sun assumed a drastically distorted reflection. A bountiful pasture still sagged under the weight of the water drops left in its wake by the morning fog. Nearby stood the stump of a dead palm tree; Timm gave it a sound kick. The worm-infested mound erupted into a foul-smelling cloud of dust. A toad family scattered in all directions. Large moths were fluttering among the structure's crumbling fibers. Johann Peter Langfoot poked around in the water with a stick. Frightened, the tattered remnants of a school of pygmy fish swam all over themselves. A droning sound started to come from the rail embankment. A switch engine was producing quite a racket. It advanced about five hundred meters and then reversed its course with a series of loud snorts. The smoke it churned out floated on in the air for quite a long while. It was too heavy to mix with the delicate cloud formations. Even its smell was stronger than all the fermenting smells of the prairie put together.

Timm came up alongside Langfoot and directed his own water down into the murky pool. Langfoot let him have it with his stick and told him that he objected to that sort of thing — even though he had caused his comrade the same displeasure a while earlier. At that they agreed to climb over the rail embankment and to explore the other half of the prairie's expanse.

A loud crunching sound could be heard coming from the gravel between the rails. But Timm said only:

"The outermost curve of the turn lies precisely at the place where we will jump aboard tonight. That's why we must break from the bushes like some sort of wild animals. Railway detectives are not lurking in every freight train. And even if they are on this one and do grab us, they're still not allowed to shoot. That's worth quite a bit, anyway. Mostly though, they're busy sleeping and quite soundly at that — there being a paycheck involved and all. And theirs is almost certainly fatter than that of the night watchman at the factory who is a compatriot of ours, incidentally, and who has found ways of accommodating a goodly number of us with shelter amid the oil drums and salt sacks for a night or two. His name is Pittje Adam. You might want to make a note of that."

There was a certain place where the field rose like a cat's back; on that spot a local mimosa tree arched its feathery branches. A green throated woodpecker hammered away at places on the *espinillo's* bark. Spunkily he ignored Timm and Langfoot as they once again landed in the grass on their stomachs. One of the two men still had a crust of bread stuck somewhere in the recesses of his sack. They divided it up fairly and gnawed on it, keeping time with one another as they did so. Timm was pleased that Langfoot had finally reached the decision to risk riding the rails. He hadn't yet said so, but his face already looked as if he would, and Timm was an expert at reading faces. Anyway most of the time they weren't faces at all, just masks. And according to Timm it wasn't clear yet whether people wore faces or masks. He turned his attention to solving this question once and for all, scratching around under his armpits as he did so, almost like an Indian. Langfoot, on the other hand, preoccupied himself with the creatures crawling around in the grass. He, too, only did so to get his own thoughts together. The sensation of a useless ego wormed its way around indecently in his brain. He too, itched everywhere, not just at the armpits like Timm. He had to scratch himself; scratching, however, didn't help him in the least.

Finally he said to Timm: "I am thoroughly fed up with the city. I may have said this often, but so help me, now I've had it up to the rafters; it's downright nauseating. I haven't any more time to keep on knocking around with this revulsion. I'm not placid enough for that. I must think again and again, not just once in a while, of how miserably the world's goods are distributed. This field here, for example, could be turned into thick beds of cucumbers or planted with tomatoes. I can hardly even remember when I last tasted a cucumber salad. That means we are lacking cucumbers. And the same situation that exists with the cucumbers we lack, but would gladly eat, exists with all the rest. Here's what I mean: we could be leading our lives with all the trappings of gods, ... and are presently informed that there is not even room enough for us to practice our skills at begging. We alone can not possibly be the only ones to blame for this. The locals also find truth in the maxim that even poverty can only be boiled in water. That's why there's got to be another unusual catch to this matter of poorly distributed goods. And that's what I'd really like to get a handle on before the Devil turns my head completely so the old swindler can pin his bag of unused tricks on me."

"It seems to me as obvious as the muck in front of us that the Devil will be quick to dispose of you before you get very far along with your decision to outwit all the fiends."

"Then I see no point in our setting off on a trip. A person will only then dislodge himself from an old comfortable spot if he entertains well-founded prospects of moving substantially ahead. Walking backwards is something I only learned to do in these parts. I could even do it with impunity because I volunteered to sweep away whatever spittle the esteemed *caballeros* fired off at the floor and at the legs of their tables.

"In this land the *gringo* is probably the most miserable and least empowered of all beings. Only for him does work become a curse and do both animate and inanimate things become repulsive. Day or night one must constantly take care to avoid misfortune so as not to have it pull the last piece of wool over one's eyes. If the field hadn't been there when needed and if the sun hadn't given me a touch of its warmth, I don't know how long I could have maintained the strength to grapple with it all and still come out ahead."

Mist was forming above the mud puddles in faint swirls. The sun had draped its face with a wine-red veil. The more distant clouds turned to saffron and scarlet. The dwellings began to dissolve in a blue haze. To preface each of its gusts the wind blew a chill that cut deep into the skin.

When they abandoned their supine position in the grass and turned into the highway to Pompeya, Timm hung his head very low. He was feeling the loss of something that had once been, even though a number of years had passed since he had owned a general store in this vicinity. At the moment, however, he dwelt on the thought that a pitcher of milk, boiling hot and rich in cream would supply the necessary counterweight to the sharp bite of the cursed winds that had descended on them from three different directions. But where could one find such a thing in a region where no one lets a milk bottle stand for more than ten seconds in front of his door?!

As if he had not noticed his friend's sadness, Johann Peter Langfoot asked, "No change of plan then? We hit the road?"

"Of course we hit the road! Not just with a hand covering our behind, either. We are traveling – though not entirely legitimately – by train. Anyway, a very big choice of ways to escape once and for all from the stench of life just isn't available."

"And may one now inquire into which direction we'll be setting off? Or is there no travel schedule for that?"

"In this case the schedule will be determined by me. That's why the direction is Northwest, and the destination is Córdoba. Understandably, it's a tentative destination. And reaching the place easily involves covering eight hundred kilometers. If we're luckier than we have been, we tear up there in a single uninterrupted stretch. And if we have absolutely no luck at all, then they'll be shoving us home in a box. In my opinion luck will be on our side this time – and outrageously so, at that.

"And now, open up your ears good and wide. If we've come to the point of jumping to our feet with a bold woop de doo, then please be so kind as to not ask me every five minutes whether we'll soon be reaching our chosen destination; that constant badgering can wrench a person's guts out. I mean, curiosity needn't always and everywhere be your trademark. Putting money on that horse is precisely what made your life go haywire. You might have come farther along if you had gone into medical quackery, especially in this part of the country and in these times generally. A better example found hereabouts of how after falling into one manure pile after another someone can still land on the grass is what you'll see when you look at my cousin. Just three years in the country and already his business is flourishing. And in his new office, complete with lusty bleached-blond nurses and chocolate-coated pastries imported from Brazil, he extracts appendices for no less than three thousand *pesos* apiece. In the last six months he has racked up two hundred of these useless appendices; please figure out for yourself what 'profit' signifies in a case like that.

"These people still actually believe in the appendix, and they pay still higher prices than that for its removal, under the right circumstances. But the most profitable business of all is being run by a man who discovered that people can live thirty years longer than normal with an enlarged pancreas. He enlarges the pancreas for no less than five thousand *pesos*. The popularity of his magical powers is enormous. And to make matters worse, to date he has had the gall not to lose a single one of his patients on the operating table.

"Frankly, of the two nags I think you'd have done better to put your money on this one. You were negligent not to, and consequently there is no reason for you to take your misery so bitterly to heart."

"Thank you, Timm, for your admonition although I haven't earned it. You see, the horse I put my money on only has periodic whims. He was born fiery while at the same time accustomed to a better diet. However, that is one item I'm not able to afford at this moment. So I pin my hopes on future moments when we'll have this hydrocephalic monstrosity of human trial and error behind us."

Above the flat roofs the circles of the street lamps swayed in a dim watery haze. The biting smell of onions and hot olive oil came gushing out from the doorways. It was already too late for the soup kitchens.

Timm sighed, "You know, my innards are growling for a juicy *Schweinebraten* today, and if there were red cabbage to go with it, then I'd have every reason to say: 'Finally a corner of paradise has come my way.' For the moment, though, it looks as if we're obliged to move out, minus the help of any celestial hosts and very much like Adam and Eve, especially like Adam, when he recognized the Woman, Eve. Nevertheless, old friend, stand straight and strong; then they can swallow us up, all right, but they'll be spitting us out just as quickly."

Passersby emerging from the city, whether from the better or the shabbier stores, or from a movie house whose long, drawn-out 'pictures' made your eyes water, your heart beat faster, and your knees weigh heavy, ... all these people had dropped the mask from their faces. They exhibited the unreal actualization of an even more unreal existence. Behind the self-induced conviction that they were laboriously concerned with harvesting the best aspects of life stood the weight of the fact that they represented nothing more than crippled forms of humanity ... weeds.

Amongst these sad shapes Timm tried to wangle a solid handout. The bugger was even successful at it. The woman who opened her purse had earlier heard a black soprano singing in church. And since she had previously assumed that Negroes only communicate in monkey language, her heart was deeply bewildered as she dispensed a one *peso* penance. An elderly man with a snow-white beard also donated twenty *centavos*. "The poor fellow is probably one of us," he said in English to his companion. To which Timm replied in the other's native language, "For that, sir, these fair God-given gifts are but too sparingly measured!" But that didn't move the distinguished gentleman in the least. He merely touched the brim of his hat. Whereupon Timm said to Johann Peter: "That goes to show you how distracted these illustrious people are. What is one to do? Every thing has its own gravity and is dependent on how the electrons spin."

Langfoot said nothing. He merely looked down at his shoes. They were full of mud. He spit to one side. A black cat crossed the road. It didn't pay to spit again. For such an animal is basically just a part of that larger "I" which unsuccessfully seeks union with Nature in order to be able to form a better world.

Chapter Five

A yellow fog, thick and mingled with smoke, was gumming up the sky. The tarp over the boxcar had a hole in it; and as they traveled, they still wanted to see the stars through the hole or at least a piece of the moon. Langfoot lay with his head on his rucksack; it smelled of mouse droppings. It was as if he lay in a field. The only things lacking were the sun and that expansive grass-imbued air that you inhale in deep breaths when moist, thick-leaved vegetation lies by a large body of water. Even though each was separately curled up in a corner, the two of them lay dangerously close to a heavy piece of machinery. Admittedly, the iron behemoth could not slide. But what if it were to slide on a stiff curve.... A person also has to think of that possibility when he is riding the rails into the unfamiliar, foggy night on a *tren de carga*. These tracks truly were made of iron. Every single thought was mashed to pure pulp by the rattling commotion they made. You could have shouted as noisily as the *Teatro Colón* orchestra, and not even the wind would have perked up its ears. And otherwise it had very keen ears.... Every shout emerging from the countryside flew in its direction. It was the wind that shouldered the burden each time a rail switch screeched under the train's grinding force. It was getting real curvature of the spine from so many rail switches. It yearned for the straightaway, for the flat pampa which it could streak through at its heart's content without any noticeable resistance. Always in competition with wheels. Like a current of water that is split in two halves and would like to press both parts together again – if only that hardness weren't in between. But the wind was a thing made up of air, and the rail cars had bent sheet metal into a form. A terrifying hoarse tone ran through the steel housing. The sound that Langfoot was picking up in his head was one he had not heard in his entire life. He had often traveled second class, sometimes even first, but never had he hopped a train without a ticket. The rucksack was only a mediocre insulator. Besides, it let the coldness in from underneath. A biting, wet, freezing cold. It sapped what little warmth there was in your extremities and tied itself like a noose around your throat.

When you don't have a watch, it's difficult to determine what hour of the night it is in a moving freight train. The *tren* had already been rolling for an eternity. It had long since left the rail switches of the city behind it. In front of it lay only the night and the next water tower. Sooner or later it's got to take on water, thought Langfoot. Sooner or later there has to be a pause following the roar. I feel a hairiness down my whole spine. I had a shave yesterday and now my beard seems to be coming out braided at the chin. These were the thoughts in which Langfoot wrapped himself. Thus ensconced he came closer and closer to sleep. By now Timm's snoring sounded like a chain saw cutting heavy lumber. He could afford to snore. His corner wasn't on the side of the wind. The scoundrel! There's one who's known for a long time how to get comfortable. Let him sleep his lousy paunch off. If only the train didn't stop.

The train stopped twice before the gray light of morning hit the plain. The two of them slept right through both stops. Their legs had become as stiff as the iron parts of the machine. Blood was only circulating in their upper bodies. It was gasping for air that kept their faces warm.

Rubbing his sleepy eyes clean, Langfoot could no longer find the hole in the tarpaulin. It was still there, but it was occluded by the fog. The fog had even quilted the insides of the boxcar – only there was no heat emanating from it. On the contrary, the temperature stood close to freezing. It was a morning frazzled with rain. Langfoot finally realized that when he was able to push a slit in the tarp slightly to the side. As for landscape, … nothing. Just the faint, useless, diagonal drizzle of the raindrops sweeping down. A fine mess. They should have slept a while longer. Timm was sleeping. Only Langfoot could no longer close his eyes. And yet the wheels were making every effort to lull his consciousness back down to size. He remained excitedly awake. He still had a ten cent bun left in his sack from yesterday's evening shopping excursion; he cut it in half and shoved it, bite by bite, between his sourly-reacting teeth. It stuck to the roof of his mouth. His tongue burned, increasing his sensation of thirst with its scratchy heat. To hell with the bread; it wasn't even honest to goodness beggar's bread!

All of a sudden the train stood still. A Quonset hut and three flatbed cars on a siding were the extent of this depot. The locomotive took on water. The boiler vents were letting some out. And Langfoot was also feeling some dreadful pressure on his bladder. But he mustn't.... He could only see that the clouds were breaking up. He saw a section of woods in the distance. The fields in the foreground were still dripping with moisture. They were now in their fourth hour of travel since the daylight rail stop. Timm seemed to be enjoying the bread. It was as if he had slept in Abraham's bosom. His face was flushed blood red. His wet hair was stuck to his temples. He spit hard into the hollow of his hand and washed himself. He stood continuously at the peep hole and counted every kilometer marker. He rambled on about a flock of sheep. He saw a herd of cattle. Thick clouds of smoke rose from an *estancia*.

Langfoot was still crouched in his corner humming a tune. Simultaneously he was rubbing his stiff knee joints.

Timm leaned back and gave him a wide smile: "I wouldn't spit on a steaming hot cup of brew right now. For the life of me, I wouldn't turn down a decent slug of *caña*." He had gotten his appetite back and furtively downed the last piece of bread. He was smacking his lips like an old, toothless cow. And with his right leg he was scratching the left.

Langfoot didn't budge. Had he been capable, he would have roundly clobbered Timm. Timm was good at heart and a person might sell his soul to the Devil for him. Just not at this particular moment. The overnight trip had put Timm in a good mood, as if he had spent a soft, warm night in a woman's company. He wouldn't stop that noisy smacking. It really seemed to give him special enjoyment. He was doing it in time to the wheels. Then he pulled out a harmonica and actually set about playing a tune. With one loud curse Langfoot promptly rained on his parade. The axles started to grind. The wheels ceased to turn so rapidly.

A small town emerged. Flat roofed dwellings. Thick coils of smoke overhead. Some cattle were lowing. Heavily laden trucks jammed the wide avenue that led into town. It appeared to be market day. Surely here the *tren* would lay over for a couple of hours. They'd be coupling and uncoupling some cars. The train was crossing a tangle of railroad tracks now. It was almost back out of town. It had actually stopped now and stood side by side with a colleague that had come from the opposite end and was waiting to take on water and coal.

Timm lifted the tarpaulin to get some air and found it clean. He jumped off the train and took care of his needs. Then he gave the other freight train the once-over, unfastened one of its doors, and stole a basket of fruit. That was a real coup. You have to have a good nose for things like that. He felt his mouth watering, pushed the basket along in front of him, and balanced it safely into the boxcar.

In it were magnificent, lemon-yellow apples. They stuffed their stomachs full of them. Within an hour they had emptied the basket of its contents and dispatched what remained of it onto a flatbed that happened to be standing in front of their noses. Timm wiped his mouth ten, maybe twenty, times with the back of his hand. The tartness of the apples had polished up his teeth. They shone like those of a monkey. His face was just as wide and plump too. A sound reached them from afar as if heavy boots were crossing the gravel. The crunching shuffled closer. It was a railroad employee parading around in his boots. Now and then he would bang with a long handled hammer against the wheels and find everything in perfect order. The hobos didn't seem to interest him. They remained crouched there with their heads down, not even daring to breathe loudly. The locomotive sounded its signal. The train had barely stayed here an hour. Steam was allowed to flow back into the cylinders, and the train eased back into motion with a groan.

"A full stomach is good for one's sleep," laughed Timm as he lay back down and began to snore again immediately. The apples had made him tipsy even though he had intestines of iron. He snored on for a while, burping now and then. It went on with fiendish regularity. Not even the wheels clicking on the rails could match the precision of his rhythm.

Langfoot's mind wandered back to his song. You could now sing at the top of your lungs in this iron monkey cage. The wheels merely devoured the notes, and between the two men and the locomotive and the wagon of the freight master lay another eighty cars or so. Measuring one kilometer in length, the train – black, diabolical, and wormlike – drew itself across the land.

The grassy plains outside seemed never to end. An endless ocean of grass. Nothing but sky and grass. The threat of rain no longer hung overhead. But the sun still had to contend with the clouds. They were flying faster than the train. The snow-white steam strove to reach them. The horizon was becoming disoriented. Already night was creeping in. The faint red hues of dusk still swept across the sky. There would again be no moon or even the minutest star.

On the second night Langfoot was considerably more successful at sleeping. The digestion process heated up his blood. His extremities lost only a little warmth. A sort of dream vision also came over him; but awakening thrust him back into merciless reality. Without giving them any warning the train had stopped. A city lay alongside the tracks and over that a frosty early morning.

The municipal police needed laborers. The authorities were inspecting the boxcars again. And along with the group of five fare-dodging passengers they apprehended came Langfoot and Timm. Sacks and cooking pots in tow they went goose-stepping through town to the *comisaría*. Bumpy, filthy streets. The people in the houses didn't even look up. But the city's security forces were quite gentlemanly and not at all militaristic. They scarcely gave the men's papers a second look. But their belongings were safely locked away. In exchange brooms, scrub brushes, and cleaning rags were distributed. The city government building had not been cleaned in four weeks. The city was being tightfisted with licensed cleaning ladies. And the local *señoritas* were saying, "No pay, no work!" What a brilliant idea it was, under the circumstances, to fall back on illegal hobos. It did everyone good to shake a leg after lying around in a contorted position for so long. The sight of them bustling about to such a degree with the cleaning equipment would have feasted the eyes of a Prussian drill sergeant. The installation glistened from top to bottom. Langfoot had cleaned the windows. On the balcony of the house across the street a woman of native Indian stock stood and smiled at him. What fiery eyes she had, the wench, and what a massive bust. It cuts right through to the marrow, straight through, when a face like that smiles. A guy has an eye for that sort of thing. And if a body were a *somebody* ... , then he might have a chance. Unfortunately window washing wasn't something you could prolong indefinitely. The constabulary supplied a thick cabbage soup, and the baker next door contributed bread rations. In the meantime evening had rolled in. In front of a movie theater the loudspeaker sang its litany, hoping to attract spectators who felt embarrassed to go to the movies so early. The fellows from the *comisaría* were really good sports; they allowed you to tell them jokes. They might also have assigned sleeping quarters if anyone had approached them about it. Now they were returning everyone's papers with an exaggeratedly grateful smile. They even revealed when the next freight train would be departing. Their only stipulation was that no one remain in town. No doubt it was a pleasant city, cut of the same cloth as its security forces. Then too there was a woman there with such a pretty way of smiling....

Of the five, four decided to continue their journey. Reportedly there still lay a bounty of such cities ahead. They sang as they made their way to the embankment where the water tank stood and the *tren de carga* had to stop. They sang like marching soldiers, including a couple of dirty stanzas in the song. Hobo verses — not sweet, but coming from the heart. Langfoot trotted along with them. Sure, he pretended to have the intention of getting on the next train with them, but actually he had gotten it into his head to stay behind. He was looking for an opportunity to run out on his comrades even though he knew that wasn't a very decent thing to do. He just didn't have a taste for traveling any more. And why shouldn't a person have a closer look at this nice town?

The fellows looked like jailbirds with their hemp sacks on their backs. And the bumpy street going down to the embankment wasn't fit for a dog. Naturally it would have been nicer if they could have undertaken a short begging spree through town. But the cordiality of the police did not go that far. Their concern was with cleanliness. The city should glisten at least as brightly as the clean swept and scrubbed government building. Truthfully there was nothing else to do but wait for the next *tren*. And Córdoba was still at least three hundred kilometers away. His interest had been piqued by the *señora's* smile and that magnificent bust. Darting around in his head there flitted not just one of his feathered fantasies but an entire cageful. They went on twittering loudly while his comrades told each other moral tales. For one, and then for a second hour the five men lay together in the weeds. Sometimes they'd steal a glance at the city, which had no more desire to settle down to sleep than they did. From time to time one of them walked up the tracks and peered southward to see if the trembling white light had come into sight yet. They were obliged to wait yet another hour. Then the thin, flickering beam began its approach emitting no sound whatsoever. It was virtually crawling along. And only when it grew larger and became increasingly more visible did the clattering of the wheels begin to follow along behind. It increased with each passing second. Another five or six minutes and their wait would be over. It was time to shoulder their bags. The wide plain was already alive with the pounding of the rails. The great goggle eyes were sweeping across the embankment. One or two more deep breaths of air and the whole thing would be over.

Langfoot was the last to approach the embankment. At the widest point of the curve he made an about-face and raced back to the city. It seemed to him that a turning point lay in this very place ... , a diving board into pressed suits and fat, black Dannemann cigars. His shadow was already gliding through the darkened acacia avenue. But the shadow and his shape were one. At that moment every lark in his head had to be alive.

Chapter Six

The streets were deplorably ill lit. Each house looked almost exactly like the next. Langfoot could simply have asked for the *comisaría*, but he still had that flock of loony ideas churning around in his head; over the years their number had grown as dense as a thicket. Even the locals had begun to notice how he would occasionally chatter out loud to himself. He continued to poke around in town, mental mayhem and all. Whom was he looking for anyway? He was the very picture of a vagabond. Was he seriously expecting to approach an Indian maiden in this outfit? Was this how he hoped to establish friendly relations with her mysterious smile? You poor fool, he laughed to himself.

He had tramped around the muddy streets for a solid hour. He had passed by the *comisaría* at least a dozen times. There were no eyes left in his head. Naturally. How can a head still be filled with sight when larks have shoved themselves before your eyes? How can a person see to find something when he doesn't know himself who he is or in what direction he's going? Judging from the pain, his knees were about to buckle. His temples were pounding. He had a stomach full of apple pulp which only further fueled his hunger for something more substantial. At last he remembered that he still had a few *pesos* in a pouch he wore slung across his chest beneath his tattered shirt. They added up to nine, the only eggs he had stowed away in his basket of savings. He had spent the last fourteen weeks trying to even the number up. But even pulling it in by the hair, that tenth *peso* couldn't be persuaded to join the others.

He found a spot under an age-old *quebracho* tree. Luckily there were no more houses nearby. He fumbled around with the pouch beneath his shirt and worked a one-spot out of it. The pouch had the warmth of his skin. A loyal soul indeed with its shiny coat of greasy fur.

Once again he made an effort to find the *comisaría*. Seven city streets simply passed beneath his stumbling feet without even bestowing one glance on him. On the other hand he did discover a small eating establishment from which emanated an odor of garlic that you could already smell from quite far away. The owner was an Italian who hadn't been assimilated yet. Inside was a low-ceilinged dining area turned raven black by smoke. A naked light bulb dangled from the ceiling illuminating a total of six people's heads. These seemed to comprise that evening's clientele. The garlic smell was coming from a leg of mutton. Langfoot sat to one side, at a place where the bulb cast no more than a dim light. He had them bring him some roast beef, but the potatoes customary with a German *Rindsbraten* had to be drawn by him on a piece of paper. Macaroni and veal Parmesan, on the other hand, came free. And with the quarter liter of red wine everything added up to seventy *centavos*. He himself was actually just a quarter satisfied. He inquired about a place where you could sleep well and inexpensively. This got him into a lengthy conversation with the host, and he was obliged to report the latest news from the provincial capital. His Spanish was no better than that of the Italians who were listening.

The host let him sleep in the tool shed that night. A horse blanket hung on a nail. A bale of corn straw lay behind the wine barrels. The sparkly red wine stood in for lullabies and cradle rocking. But the accursed wheels of that freight train still rattled across his mind. A person wanting to stretch out for a few winks with a pleasant dream doesn't travel Pullman first class without a reason.... No, not a smidgeon of Langfoot's dream is to be aired here.

The morning looked even more dismal than the night before. Langfoot washed up under the pump. The few hairs on his head were boring their way inward and drowning out the chirping of his birds. The owner came along and inquired as to his well-being. He knew now whom he was dealing with, and he offered him a job in exchange for food, drink, and a place to sleep. Langfoot accepted on condition that he be allowed to go to town on an errand. Naturally his errand concerned the smiling woman of whom he had dreamed extensively that night. He could no longer eradicate her from his thoughts. Something madonnalike emanated from her. No doubt she has a dozen children clinging to her apron, he thought. She must still be wiping away the snot from the youngest three and have a husband who walks woodenly through life not knowing any more how or where to warm up. Wearing passably clean shoes and without the prisoner's bag on his shoulders, Langfoot went back to stumbling through the streets.

A small city – humming like a beehive with activity. *Quebracho* woods stood nearby. The wheels and conveyer belts of the sawmills were furiously rattling away. An acrid smell blanketed the city. Small children were peeling movie posters from the fences. The *lechero* was selling his fresh warm milk right from the cow's udder. And had it been possible, the fruit salesman would have loaded the whole orange grove right onto his cart too. As it was, though, he had to be satisfied with a pair of leafy boughs from a pale green lime tree. Langfoot caught a glimpse of himself in the mirror of a shop specializing in fine men's wear. He concluded that he looked decent enough for a backward town like this. There remained, of course, not the least trace of a pleat in his trousers; he never had placed much value on vanities of that sort. But the wine-red wool vest under the gray coat provided just the right touch. Had he topped things off with a pair of glasses, he might perhaps have been mistaken for the spice dealer's assistant. He was certainly equally capable of distinguishing mint from chamomile, fennel from arnica, and spurge from horsetail. It was the kind of job on which a person could still lay his hands if a tangible opening could ever be uncovered among the competition. But for the moment what Langfoot wished at all costs to do was uncover the smiling madonna. He didn't smell the cheese odor and stench of garlic that clung to his jacket. The women, who were returning from the *feria,* didn't even look in his direction. The thought crossed his mind that he should be careful not to let the mud puddles anoint his shoes. It was already quite enough for his nose still to be plugged up with the sand that the wind had flung into his rail car. He imagined a plump, naked arm curling itself around his neck. He was hoping to get into the right mood. On a poster he saw Greta Garbo playing Mata Hari. It occurred to him that he had seen the real Mata Hari dance at the Wintergarten in Berlin. A real fashion plate. A beautiful, exotic woman. A suntanned body that could slither and curl like a snake. No resemblance to the nordic white and ice-cold Garbo. Especially not in the face. Mata Hari had a Javanese profile, which the smiling madonna resembled far more. It was the madonna he sought. It was the madonna he wished to visit. He furled himself around the house like a flag. He bought himself a newspaper and stationed himself with it at the corner. He stood reading the paper very attentively while also peering far up and over it at a certain window. He was poked in the ribs by the singing used-bottle dealer, who growled "Oops!" in his direction. But he didn't comprehend. A couple of cars also drove by splattering filth. This is monstrous! God, am I a pig, or what? he said to himself. He had just thought back to the first and last visit he had paid to a black woman.

It had been in Rio on that notorious street with the sky-high royal palms on a smelly canal. He had been standing on this corner for two hours now. A little girl brought him a loaf of white bread. He held it in his hand for a long time not knowing why. It did not occur to him to wonder whose charitable heart he might have touched to that extent. The thinking reflexes of his brain only fell into gear much later. Shame instantly overcame him. He took off then and there and told the restaurant owner he wanted to stick around.

Now he was on his feet from six in the morning until twelve at night. He swept the blackened dining room. The dishes he was supposed to wash were so greasy they'd stick together. He had lost his taste for red wine. There was a swollen rat floating dead in a half empty barrel in the cellar. The proprietor was a real lout, who uttered dreadful oaths in his Neapolitan dialect.

Every Friday night there was a friendly little fistfight at the eatery. It hinged on the differing Spanish and Italian philosophies concerning wine varieties, meat dishes, and older versus younger women. The surrounding neighborhood took no further notice. The movie theaters were filled to the rafters on evenings like those. Langfoot stood behind the counter and rinsed glasses. Langfoot stood over the stove cooking up spaghetti and macaroni. Langfoot mixed together pork and mutton, tomatoes and olives, onions and paprika into a special goulash. Langfoot was constantly fishing dead rats out of the wine barrels.

It was all over with the madonna's smile. But why shouldn't there be other similarly plump beings in this pleasant metropolis, who might occasionally honor the establishment of Cesare Vandotti with a visit? Depending on the circumstances, a dyed-in-the-wool Neapolitan woman is preferable to an Indian woman. Not all of them have hair on their upper lip and brass wagon wheels hanging from their ears that prevent you from nibbling on their cute rosy earlobes. Furthermore, he could follow the example of his boss Cesare Vandotti. A connoisseur of the flesh. An athlete among skirt chasers. The kind of guy who couldn't be put under a table or out of a bed. But Langfoot was still too much of a greenhorn on this turf. The specter of the *gringo* always stood in one's way. He still hadn't gotten the hang of things. A person didn't even have the time to properly comb his hair. And to top it all off, business was bad – appallingly bad. This dreadful decline in business was a new symptom of the times. It was as infectious as an epidemic of cholera or of the plague. Yet at the same time there were people who managed to become round as a ball. Like the master shoemaker who came in every evening and spent three *pesos* on rum and dice games. Or those, as it happened with *señora* Bugatti, who were able to do business in paper, mops, eau de cologne, house shoes, and chocolate. At nine o'clock her store shutters went down; at nine thirty her combination platter of onions, vegetables, and stockfish had to be on the table. During the first week she had never left a tip ... , because Langfoot had not been allowed to wait on her. Only the boss himself had the honor. It was not until the third week that Langfoot noticed she was wearing red nail polish and therefore must be verging on her forty-third Indian-summer year of life. Furthermore he noticed that she washed herself with a soap that gave off a very repulsive odor and that she was a widow. An imposing figure in the eyes of someone who had once been somebody but who no longer had any importance or even enjoyed a square meal. A very cuddly sort of person. In all probability she kept a feisty angora cat in bed with her at night. And then again it could just as easily be an ordinary field, forest, or meadow cat. But in the end the cat lost out to Langfoot.

For one week, three weeks, five weeks Langfoot had it made. The turning point seemed actually to have been reached. For the first time in three years he was back to wearing a pale yellow cotton jersey, matching collar attached, and a checkered, red-and-white tie. His one regal suit of clothes could easily have been multiplied had he placed great value on such things. Or had the hard heart melted inside his breast and the birds in his head forgotten how to sing. But *señora* Bugatti bore no resemblance to a smiling madonna. She turned out more like a pair of pincers. His strength was not up to the challenge. He was consuming five times the amount of meat that was normally good for his stomach. When he shaved a mangy billy goat smirked back at him in the mirror. The urge to stretch gave way to horror stories. When he felt an itch on his lips, it was the exhalations of a toothless mouth he smelled. To sedate himself he drank tincture of bromural. He didn't ultimately get the boot, just three used cardigans belonging to her late departed husband, a pair of knee boots that were two sizes too small, and a wallet-size picture of Saint Hieronymus. Afterwards she still wanted to remain a valued guest at Cesare Vandotti's pub. After all, it was the only Neapolitan establishment in town. That was something in which Langfoot no longer put any stock. He had thirty-two *pesos* in his pouch. On the other hand he also had an ugly rash all over his body. He was fed up with the rats. He was fed up with all the toothless garlic mouths. He had not seen very much of the city.

One evening about the hour the train had sped off with his companions but without him, he sat crouching under the water tanks alongside the embankment again waiting for the flickering light to start its approach. The summer air was balmy. The mood spreading across the wide expanse was such that there was truly not anything else a person could do but travel another stretch further into the savanna. He had no way of suspecting that it would burst into a massive fire.

Chapter Seven

The long and thorny grass that had burned to ashes on the savanna blew skyward at the slightest touch, tried to raise itself into a cloud, and fell back powerlessly as dust upon the crusty black earth. In a gorge the heat remaining from the rapidly moving fire would flare up sporadically. The air was too dry to absorb it, and the wind was incapable of escaping from the power of the flames. An endless surface, spread practically across half the horizon, was still struggling with the yellow, crackling, and consuming scourge. The sap of the plant stalks was being transformed into a gray vapor. The upward motion took on an increasingly darker hue, forming a heavy layer of moisture between the destructive horror and the still blue sky above. A pungent smell imposed itself on each breath of air; the palate and tongue dried out. The eyes turned red as they succumbed to their owner's irresistible desire to scratch them. At times a person's sight was affected; then the landscape would take on a variety of grotesque shapes, the air filled by a ghostly tremor.

The stillness of the grave lay heavy upon the burned steppe. The *ñandús* were the first to flee before the rapidly approaching fire. Hordes of swallows, quail, and ant-eating magpies quickly followed their lead. Their squawking had also stirred up the guanacos, the armadillos, and the black wild hogs. In the panic-stricken whirlwind of their flight from the hellish jaws of the heat and from the tongues of flame that hissed horizontally across the land the sparrow hawks suddenly emerged, followed by the bare-necked and yellowish-brown, feathered vultures. They were pecking at the bodies of the small rabbits, snakes, and wild horses that remained scattered around. They had to hurry and were leaving the partially dismembered bodies behind in the stifling heat, some still bleeding and twitching. The heat in turn instantly transformed these into the same grayish-white ash as it had the thorny collar of the wild pineapple, the thistle bushes, the dock and spurge plants, and the narrow leaved sedge.

Only the reeds of the lagoons survived the onrushing wall of fire. They had curled up around the outer edges and lay under a thin layer of airborne ash dust bending thirstily toward the slimy water. Frogs stood with gaping mouths on creeper leaves the size of a man's palm. Pygmy fish would suddenly emerge like shiny blue, red, and yellow butterflies. A yacaré stretched his reptilian head out, goggle-eyed, from a clump of matted rushes. Dragonflies hung in grapelike clusters from the branches of a crippled willow. Several times the cicadas began to chirp, and then abruptly ended their song again after the first few notes as if the air were still too fragile to be able to spin the glistening thread to its conclusion.

Time had stood still for quite a while. Even the sun seemed fastened to a milky haze out of fear. It had pulled in its plumage of rays and almost resembled the moon when it has climbed into the sky a couple of hours too soon and must conceal its matte, amorphous disc from the bright day. But when at last it occurred to the sun, its fixtures now muted, to glide back downwards, evening had already arrived. It had taken into its fold all the bitterness of the dead grasses. It surged heavily like a wave across the gradually fading surfaces. A bluish shimmer rose languidly from the ground up to meet it. The sun was dripping blood; it still had a long way to go before reaching those black abysses of the night that were opening up behind the cloudlike mass of the Cordillera. But the night became no real night. It stayed gray and hazy and gave the full moon an equally short life as it worked its way up out of a distant lagoon staring absently at the sky and blowing a bit of cool air before it. Like an aquatic animal it had emerged, taken a breath of air, and disappeared.

Northwest on the horizon a raven black cloud had suddenly appeared. Its erratic approach was massive and ungainly. Along the edges it glimmered in green and sulfuric yellow. Sparks flew from its fat stomach. Now it was the heavens that seemed to want to burn, much as the earth had done hours before. A dull pounding, a roar like what might be heard behind closed and thickly upholstered doors, tried convulsively to break out. Any minute now the rolling and raging might cause the cloud to burst apart. It had swollen up so by now that it covered half the sky. The air flew whistling beneath it and stirred the dust upwards. Mountains of dust pushed against the heavy weight of the cloud. The three ranches that seemed to have pulled together in the uncertain light disappeared into a gorge made up of blackness, sulfur, and circulating ashes. The cicadas no longer even attempted the slightest note. On the lagoon the reeds straightened up again in fear of yet another disaster. Even the water, which stood blue-gray and lit only from below, didn't move. Frogs and fishes crouched in the mud as if an eternal sleep lay before them. The foliage on the plain stood still and listened to the sultry heat with the ears of a mouse.

The pitiful screech of a young magpie caught in the intertwined vegetation was the first thing to suddenly break the silence. And so, as if it had allowed itself to be ignited by this sudden outcry of fear, the wind turned a few times on its own axle and blew outward in every direction. It made deep furrows across the ashen debris of the land. It burrowed into the dust, tore itself out again trailing a long streamer, and wrapped this around itself. It had the shape of a cloud and cozened up fraternally to the real cloud inside the thick billowing haze. At last wind and cloud were one. The lightening drew its greatest power of illumination from this union and allowed its crackling bolts to flash far and wide. As these collided with darkness, thunder was released. With the wind behind them the warring elements made for each other like arrows. Sparks spewed forth. From within the ever mightier cacophony the first raindrops came clattering down, mixed with hailstones the size of pigeon eggs. Night enveloped herself in her blackest coat of darkness. Serpentine lightning bolts rent it in two. There was no more resistance to the rain storm anywhere on the land, or above, or below. It thoroughly disgorged itself in a driving vertical downpour. At first the singed and clogged pores of the earth could hardly absorb it, as though even the ashes left after the fire could not come together with their antagonist Brother Water. Lake upon lake grew in circumference, and the flow spread across ever wider surfaces. But all of a sudden the resistance of the ashen coating relented and succumbed to the weight. Furrows opened up, swallowed the streams, filled up a second time, expanded in width, took on greater depth, became brooks and ultimately raging river beds. The entire plain was crisscrossed by a host of more than a million such flood canals. The flood surged all the way to the hills and nearly stood at the cleared fields of an estate called *Estancia Santa Teresina*. An immeasurable surface lay under water. All traces of the range fire were erased. Only if a person took a deep breath of chilly air did the sharp aroma of singed dock weed still scratch the tongue.

On the road from the lagoon, making a beeline for the first *rancho*, staggered the nearly unrecognizable silhouette of a man. At times when lightning lit his profile, one could see that it could only be Langfoot's sharp nose that protruded to that degree frontward from the face.

Langfoot had crouched in the reeds of the lagoon while the savanna burned. Here he knew that fire could not touch him. He had been hunting for turtles. When he finally saw their old shriveled faces, he was overcome by a dreadful shudder. He was so hungry that his teeth gnawed on panicle. The magnificence of both range fire and storm over the hot ash had enriched him with a new and stirring experience.

Chapter Eight

My experience with turtles has been the same as with the pock-marked Indian women who are approaching one hundred. The Bible has been exhorting us to respect our elders all these years, but as long as we're supposed to bend our knee and lower our voice, then it ought to be before something that inspires respect in us, not something that teaches our blood to curdle, thought Langfoot as he allowed the archaic grandmother turtles to continue paddling around in the mud of the lagoon. It was a crazy idea to begin with, honing one's appetite with the idea of roast turtle without having a side dish. Not even the juicy root of some club moss or the leaf of a plantain.

Again he aimed his nose straight ahead ignoring the hopelessly impoverished-looking *rancho* and making his way to the cattle rancher's *estancia*. Enough heat to suffocate a bear still hovered in the air, and the hot sand was cooking off the puddles that had been left by the rainstorm. His shoes were soaking up water, and the weight of his heel was pressing it back out. Pleasant music to the ears. It was a beat you could march to. He was obliged to plod along for another full hour with this unusual music in his shoes. The eye no longer did such a good job of measuring distances on the savanna. Furthermore, other than a couple of lame-looking poplar trees riddled by the fire, there wasn't any other reference point out there. Not even the glassy expanse stretching out between them knew for sure how far they lay from one another. Langfoot jumped across a narrow irrigation ditch. Here began the land that men had made arable. Here, every so often, you could see fences unfurling. Harvested cornfields brightened the landscape with shades of yellow and rust red. Frogs were doing their best to liven up an otherwise voiceless, endless silence. And Langfoot thought it advisable to clean his shoes a little. The leaves of the weeds worked just like shoe brushes. That was one trick he knew. He beat the dust out of his trousers with a tough stick from a thistle bush. He didn't really want to approach a local resident looking like the Devil himself.

Behind the fifth fence a herd of cattle was proudly milling about in shades of black and white and slate gray. A surly group indeed. It didn't even take notice of a human who had never before come in touch with it. There were about five hundred cows. Their heavy udders nearly skimmed the ground. Definitely a dairy farm. There had to be an owner here who knew how to specialize. The management couldn't be terribly wealthy, but still. The walls of the maple brown stalls gave off white reflections. Straw and hay flowed from the open sheds; these stretched all the way to the dwellings of the peons. There were four of these houses, each separate, unfenced, and a hundred feet from the next – as if people weren't getting along or wanted to look like scaled-down gentleman gardeners. It also looked as if no one put any value on organization of any type. Indeed, the first shack stood in an abandoned garden, and at the entrance stood two black sows having a quarrel.

At one corner a broad cactus had ensconced itself. Langfoot detected that old familiar prickly sensation in his knees, and his first impulse was to dust off. He'd have given a *peso* just to get his hands on a cigarette. He had to be satisfied with a cactus thorn. He sucked on the hardened wood as if it were full of golden-yellow Virginia tobacco. He wondered whether there was any value at all to demeaning himself here with the lowlife. Or should he put it all on the line and present himself to the management? A self-respecting man will take his chances with the higher ups – his equals, as it were. And if the wind is blowing too harshly, there is always the hinterland to fall back on. There always remains the informality of one impoverished nobody speaking to another in the same boat.

He was strongly inclined to opt for the dwellings that befit his own station. He argued with the birds in his head for a while longer. One of them always wanted to come out above the other. A white rage surged through him. Damn! He had very nearly swallowed the cactus thorn when someone jabbed him in the side with a hoe of some kind. This is not the kind of merry greeting one experiences every day. Especially not when a certain girl feels like laughing herself to death over one's skittishness. Langfoot had no other choice but to burst out laughing right along with her. He laughed until his stomach ached. The girl reached down with the hoe and pulled him up. There. He was back on both legs again. And he was peering into a face that had still not quite finished laughing. He asked her if his appearance was really strange enough to make a person laugh herself silly. Actually, he told her, he was in no mood to laugh. A pitcher of milk would decidedly be preferable, and if a man were able to settle down in that corner of the world for a while, he said, then his troublesome journey might not have been in vain.

She wiped away the signs of laughter, leaned on her hoe, and didn't utter a sound. He noticed that she had a wide, greasy mouth and that a gray cornea blinded her left eye. The hair hung shaggily about her head, as if even the word 'comb' might be unknown to her. Her feet stood naked in a pair of oafish shoes, and her dress had not the slightest trace of color left in it. It hung loosely from her narrow shoulders like something cut from a feed bag.

"You could have prodded me a whole lot sooner, little sister. You've certainly had plenty of time to determine that I look like a human being. A brassiere would certainly do wonders for your figure, my dear. I have disliked overly buxom women for some time now. My name is Langfoot, by the way, Johann Peter Langfoot. And the name you go by is another something you owe me."

Her eyes rolled back into another fit of convulsive laughter. Giggling, she gave him a jab with her elbow and said, "You seem to me to be just the right man. A man such as you has never come my way as long as I can remember. Where on earth have you been keeping yourself all this time? My name is Henrietta. And feel free to speak German with me, if you like. You have that look about you too."

"I certainly would not have taken you for a native *criolla*. Therefore let's talk the way we're accustomed to. I find you attractive. But if you want me to find you even more attractive, just don't forget that pitcher of milk. I was out duck hunting. I came into the hands of murderers and thieves. They took the very tent out from under my behind. Are you married? What are your toddlers up to? Can a person speak German with your husband? Don't make me extract everything like a dentist pulling teeth!"

"You ask more questions than any grandmother ever answered during her entire lifetime. I have no children, and my sister is the one who will be having a wedding month after next. If you keep up this comedy routine, maybe my father will let himself be talked into giving you shelter for the night. Go right on in. I still have a way to go."

She gave him one more jab with the hoe and ran to the other side of the bumpy roadbed. She remained standing behind the hedge for a while looking back at him as he pushed along toward the house, skirting the fence, and shaking his head as he went.

He came to a stop at the open door and yelled out, "Good evening!" Someone beckoned to him from inside. He ducked and found himself standing in a large, square room. The small windows allowed little light to enter. He noticed a fireplace and a scrap of meat on the spit. He felt a pleasant tickle in his nose. A woman was stirring something in a pot, and at the table reading a newspaper sat the old man who had beckoned to him. With his spectacles halfway down his nose he gave Langfoot a long look. Langfoot stared right back at him. The wood fire was crackling. The roasting meat gave off a hissing sound.

Langfoot reckoned that it was up to him to speak first. He shifted his weight from one foot to the other and began to mumble, "It's a joy on finding oneself this close to the ends of the earth to come across people from back home. I spoke with Henrietta. She said I might get a pitcher of milk here. There was also some mention of finding shelter for the night. This is my fifth week on the road. I am a naturalist by profession, but I'm handy with a saw too. It would be hilarious if our kind were not to get a paying job at least once in a while."

The soup in the pot continued to bubble. The meat was smelling better all the time. The woman stood there one arm braced on her hip, and the old man kept shoving his glasses back up his nose. Langfoot saw him raise his shoulders a little. The woman shook her head. That seemed to be all the answer his speech would get. The situation slowly turned awkward. There was nothing else for him to do but ask if a person could take a seat. He blamed his aching knee joints. A memento from the war. He proceeded to pull a chair out for himself. It was actually more like a stool, roughly hewn from pine wood. He sat there, cross-legged, like some sort of idol. He opened his mouth again, and this time he opened it wider. His tale wore on for a whole extra quarter of an hour. Finally the old man stood up. Langfoot didn't let him stand by himself. They stood facing one another. The old man extended his hand. The woman also came up and gave Langfoot her hand. It was slightly sticky from stirring, a really sprawling hand. And with that everything was taken care of that has to be done for someone in this part of the world to be able to stretch his legs out beneath another man's table and eat with him.

The woman had placed four bowls on the table. But everybody still seemed willing to wait for Henrietta. Undoubtedly the other girl who kept continually hanging around the fire was the sister. Her name was Carlotta. As for the old man who looked like the father of the two sisters, he signed himself Joan Ribbensahm, native of Siebenbürgen, resident of this locality going on thirty-four years now. Langfoot learned this much before he was at last allowed to guzzle down the promised pitcher of milk. But Henrietta didn't show up until he had taken a hearty bite out of the meat. It tasted like peat marinated in bouillon cubes, and it stuck to your teeth. They stayed busy the rest of the evening picking strands of it out from between their teeth.

It was agreed that Langfoot could help out with the building of two new irrigation ditches. The old man was kind of an inspector on the *estancia*; to use the term 'foreman' would have been inaccurate. They agreed Langfoot was to earn one *peso* and a half. Meals were to be taken here in the house, and they still had to arrange a place for him to sleep. They settled on the storage room in the loft. There had been pigeons in there a couple of years before. Feathers and excrement still imbued the place with their smell and stickiness. But there was enough straw there to be used as both a mattress and a quilt.

The dirt where the ditch was being dug was a soft clay imbedded with gravel stones. The weight of the spade multiplied with each hour of work. After two days the clumsy stick would practically gnaw blisters into a man's hands. The time it took for lunchtime to roll around when you clocked in at seven seemed pitifully long. Your stomach growled, and the sun took no mercy on any skin that was as yet unaccustomed to the air currents prevalent at those latitudes. The two girls were not lazy at the table. Not with their teeth and not with their chatter. Langfoot was having trouble keeping pace with them. In the process he became downright sleepy. No one would begrudge him an hour of shuteye. My Lord! There was an awful stench in that narrow storage room! And the timekeeping was no less stringent during the afternoon. The old man had eagle eyes! The four of them would stand out in a field digging one meter ditches. Sometimes Henrietta would come over and bring each of them a pitcher of milk. Langfoot would run his shredded skin over the cool surface of the crock.

As for the girls, the old man kept an eye on them as if they too were a chunk of time that mustn't be frittered away idly. At first they weren't even a consideration where Langfoot was concerned. As soon as he had satisfactorily filled his belly, he would shamble all over the *estancia* with that curious face of his, focusing most of his interest on the newly planted crop of *mate*. In fact this crop was not even inside old Ribbensahm's section any more. Responsibility for it lay in the hands of Foreman Bruckmann.

It was on this occasion that Langfoot also learned that the owner of the *estancia* was a Swiss fellow with only one remaining daughter, a girl with prospects of inheriting every last thing on the property. A daughter and an inheritance – these were not altogether unpleasant words to hear. On another occasion Langfoot asked whether the daughter was already engaged to someone; an arrangement made by her relatives, as it were? But the daughter was not promised to anyone as yet. She didn't like any of the local boys, and compatriots able to strike her fancy turned up less frequently here than grasshoppers did in some years.

The birds were swarming through Langfoot's head. They were starting to make another ruckus. They did set one thought straight in his mind. Like a gusting wind he swirled into every nook and cranny carrying this new thought with him. He frittered away the rest of the evening roaming through the fields, the storage sheds, and the large barnyard. He was wearing the wine-red wool vest beneath the gray jacket again. The young lady had piqued his curiosity. He heard her playing the piano. And whenever she rode through the fields with her father, he would crouch in a ditch with the salty taste of sweat on his tongue.

In the end Henrietta had managed to find Johann Peter attractive. This caused him to forget the young lady. He and Henrietta would sometimes stand together under the prickly cactus. They squeezed one another the way people do who know that one thing leads to another when their blood starts to boil. She asked him if he liked her better than Carlotta. For she had no knowledge as yet of the young lady at the ranch. Actually she knew a lot about the girl, but not that Langfoot had convinced himself he would eventually be able to fool around with the young lady as much as he now could with her.

Langfoot said, "The word *love* should not be spoken as loudly as you said it a minute ago. We should only think it. I often think of your white teeth. And also of how you can go on watching a man be forced to beg you for the least bit of body heat when he has legs as straight as mine and a head of hair that isn't strewn with chaff. You're wearing a dress that smells of chimney smoke and cow stalls. But I'd like to know what things smell like under that dress."

She dealt him such a mighty blow that he flew into the prickly bushes. What an odd way to answer, he thought, and rubbed his back. She extracted one of the thorns from his shoulder kissing him behind the ear as she did so. That was his most sensitive area. Had the choice been his, he'd have headed upstairs immediately with her over his shoulder. But Carlotta was posted outside the door with her ears to the wind. They didn't give her the pleasure.

At dinner time the old man said, "Peter, my friend, tomorrow you can help out at the *mate* plantation. The hired hand took off. That's because I put some extra leather on his hide. Furthermore, the young Miss loaned me her riding crop to do it with. The lady has also been asking about you, ... what sort of person you might be, and all."

Not put together much differently from the guy you thrashed, thought Langfoot. But he didn't say it out loud. He just looked at Henrietta. Using the tip of her tongue, she was intent on retrieving the scraps of meat caught between her teeth. She had a tongue that was small, agile, perpetually moist, and snakelike. Her lips were about to pop, they were so flushed with blood. It's been a good while since a man has kissed them or tried to guess the weight of your hair by taking it in his hand, hasn't it?

Langfoot lay in the straw waiting for Henrietta. Admittedly, it was not yet bedtime. But the old man was on his way to the owner's place; it was time to go over accounts and for each to have his say about the winter crop. Under the right circumstances that might last an eternity.

For that reason alone Henrietta ought to come see him for an hour or so. Why shouldn't they take advantage of such a splendid opportunity? Make a little haste, Henrietta!

Her breath moved across his face like a swarm of insects. The taste was one he hadn't experienced for a long time. He wished she would remain energetic like this with him for the whole, long, sweet night.

At the same time he was quietly dozing off. And by the moonlight that came clambering down from the skylight searching the storeroom for a choice morsel Langfoot's face even managed to look passably young and fresh.

The wee hours of dawn, however, led thoughts of the young miss to cross his mind again. He had since found out that her name was Paulina and that she was anything but prudish. He just wasn't having any luck tracking her down, though. He had already been smacked three times by the boss because he wouldn't quit that nosy poking around of his.

He was quite an oddball, the boss. He behaved as if a peon were less significant than a pile of dung in the barnyard ... or less than a thistle by the fence. And yet he, Langfoot, had let himself be slapped around without complaining. Not only that, but he had said, "Excuse me!" That had probably irked the old louse even more. With those icy gray sideburns he looked like a mature Kaiser Franz Joseph. Almost every afternoon he could be seen marching across the fields for an hour or two with the shotgun. Sometimes Miss Paulina would keep him company. And sometimes she also played the piano. Then Langfoot would crouch under the window and, out of pleasure, give every bird in his head permission to sing; ... because the lady could play Schubert and Chopin so delightfully. Naturally, her delightful playing was something about which he'd much rather have spoken to her eye to eye.

He could have spoken to her about it when he was told to take a basket full of yams to the kitchen the next morning. There she stood, fresh and scented, stirring a pudding and wearing a yellow dress that reminded him of an acacia. Right away she flew into his face with an oath because he had not wiped off his dirty shoes. God! He simply wasn't accustomed to crossing a floor that was as shiny as a mirror any more. And he might very well have given an appropriate answer to her oath. But the cook – the brown bitch – positioned herself squarely between them with her fat hindquarters. On top of that a mastiff snarled at him from under the stove.

Paulina was simply delicious. With arms that seemed carved from a single piece of ivory. He found it impossible to tear his eyes away from hers. She, for her part, was convinced that someone needed to get a handle on this strange fellow. "You're Carlotta's new boyfriend, I suppose," she asked "or is it Henrietta's? What kind of a German *Landsmann* are you?"

"Roughly speaking I'm from the Rhine, Ma'am, where they operate production lines and braid electrical cable. And where five feet from wherever you are there's either a smokestack or a steeple."

"And I'll bet it hasn't been ten years since you came, right?"

"I might feel better if I had been here at least three. What's been happening hereabouts hasn't counted for much. So far I've held one losing hand after another. Over time not even a horse could put up with that, Miss. Only when I hear you play the piano do I start to feel better. You should play more often."

"For you? You do seem to be a strange bird! Do you always have funny notions like that?"

"Sometimes they're downright inspired. But it's pointless to let any leave my skull. For whose benefit?"

"We could discuss all that sometime. Maybe tomorrow night. Then you could come clean the fireplace over here. And if you polish it up nicely, I might play you some music. Don't stare at me like that all the time. Go ahead and have your Carlotta. She's a quick, hard-working girl. Actually, she's still too good for the likes of you."

"There's nothing between Carlotta and me. And there's nothing happening with Henrietta either. There isn't a thing going on between me and anybody. Nothing to relish, that is. I'm just traveling through. I've been on the road for an eternity already. I might have reached my destination sooner if something trivial didn't always hold me up. Sordid trivialities are positively hounding my trail. And if you looked me squarely in the eye, you'd know who I truly am."

Miss Paulina gazed sideways at Langfoot for a long time. His own eyes were planted in some corner, and he didn't know where to rest his hands. No matter what their position, they seemed to be in his way. The nervous sort, pondered Paulina. What an unusual stranger this was.

She frowned a little adding a brusque note to her voice that didn't ring true. "How is it you can stand around here for so long, Mister? I told you specifically enough that you were not to scour our stove until tomorrow evening. Out!" The hand movement she made flew through the air like a rock.

Langfoot dodged the blow. In so doing, he struck his head against the china cabinet. The porcelain tinkled inside. He felt the painful, pulsating vein in his temples and clenched his teeth. Only a grunt came out though it was supposed to have been a word.

Out in the vegetable garden he sat squatting under a tree until he finally let his feet slide out and lay for a long time in the grass. The sun stroked his face. The warmth brushing over his skin soothed him.

Suddenly he had to laugh out loud. The birds in his head were playing another good for nothing trick on him.

He lay in the grass until noon. The gardener in charge of the *mate* crop might come along then and surprise him in this lethargic state. A nice reprimand would then be in order. But he didn't come. And Langfoot had finally made up his mind not to scrub the stove. What does that snooty kid take me for, anyway? I may look like an all-round failure. But only according to my standards. People can make a circle around me as wide as they do around a smelly dung heap. But only the fate I've dished out for myself has that right. Not you, you flesh and blood cactus. You barbed spike!

He didn't go to lunch. He poked around down by the lagoon. The dragonflies hovered motionless and glasslike in the warm air. They looked like neon flowers with no stem. A fire-red butterfly hung, its wings tired from flying, under a cluster of mimosa. The *espinillo* trees could scarcely withstand the weight of the big, green flies.

Langfoot started to collect small, flat stones and hurl them across the surface of the water. They would skip at least twelve times before going under. That made him happy. That relaxed him. As loudly as possible he swore a vulgar oath. It was a reference to what some call *existence*. "There you have it!" But the birds in his head were there too after all.

That night he waited for Henrietta in the straw again. She brought the smell of carnations with her. He allowed himself to be kissed behind the ear again. She said 'yes' to everything he wanted. After a while he asked her, "If I were to say to you now, 'Henrietta, when shall we get married?' What kind of a reply would you have for that? I have nothing. You have nothing. And what our union produces should, according to the simplest rules of mathematics, have even less. Do you think it's worth it then?"

"Marriage and you!" laughed Henrietta.

"Why do you have such a low opinion of me? I may not know whether your father will still have any work cut out for me in the morning, or better yet, whether he will still be allowed to give it to me, but the time could very well come again when I get it into my head to build myself a house. And where there's space enough for one individual with his lazy behind, surely a couple of them and their dependents should have enough space as well. Nothing dies out in the world. Everything has its own immortality."

Her lips remained tightly sealed when she laughed. For she was afraid that the old man might hear her downstairs if she burst out laughing. That was what she'd have preferred to do. And beyond that silly smothered giggle not another word came from her mouth.

She had lain beside him all night. She stayed there even when he got up. The old man was already banging around downstairs. It was time to go to work, and it was high time that everyone get a decent breath of air.

Carlotta stood at the bottom of the stairs cocking her head upward. She winked at him and said, "Sleep warm and well last night?"

He winked back at her, "Slept very well. It was just a little sultry. A storm is probably on its way."

She tapped him lightly on the cheek. And that was when he noticed that she had the same aroma about her as Henrietta. Perhaps she'll also laugh the same silly way when asked whether she'd find an early wedding agreeable. Actually what she really needs is for someone to come along who'll take a bite of this crabapple.

He'd lost his taste for work. He muddled around with the poles and boards as if he had never in all his life done that kind of work. The gardener kept shaking his head but didn't say anything. He let Langfoot be.

Sometimes Langfoot would stand for a long time and search the sky. It was cloudless, and the wind was sleeping somewhere in a sedge swamp along with the great-grandmother turtles. Or at other times Langfoot would busy himself with the spade as if he must catch up on seven years of wasted time. Torn roots were flying in every direction, and the flies were crawling into the darkest recesses of the foliage. The situation with Langfoot seemed increasingly strange to the gardener. He observed how the dripping wet hair was sticking to his temples. He must be planning to talk to the old man before the day was over. If you got right down to it, the crazy *gringo* was just too high strung.

At seven, when it had became cooler among the trees, Langfoot made his presence known in the kitchen and reported for the stove cleaning job. The Indian woman grinned at him, her scraggly black hair dangling above her eyes. She didn't respond to his announcement, nor did she offer him a chair so he could take a seat. Langfoot turned around and took a good look at the crockery and the shiny brass kettles in various sizes. He raised his nose. Coming from the oven was the aroma of fresh baking. His mouth was beginning to water. On the table lay a partially eaten loaf of bread. Hardly bothering to ask for permission, he tore a piece off for himself and stuffed his cheeks full. He almost choked when Miss Paulina was suddenly standing in front of him. She was amused by his rapid chewing. She said that cleaning the stove was not so urgent and wondered whether he wanted to go catch frogs with her at the lagoon. The boss had an urge for baked frog legs. She was wearing a tight-fitting, coarse cloth dress and boots that were laced all the way to her calves.

Langfoot answered, "A person does what he's told. Catching frogs has also been one of my lines."

They went down to the lagoon. Langfoot already had every shrub and clump of reeds down here thoroughly memorized. He was carrying a metal bucket and net. Paulina was walking two, three steps ahead and was deftly swinging her hips.

The water's uppermost skin was murky and foul smelling. The turtles were sticking their heads upward. The great-grandmother frogs with their fat yellow tummies were stretched out on the large leaves croaking so loudly that a person could often not understand his own words. The bucket could have been filled with this fat lot in a matter of ten minutes. But Miss Paulina was of the opinion that the meat on these older creatures had a soapy taste. We'd do better to abide by the younger generation.

She sat down on one of the burned out anthills atop a towering black *tacuru* mound and left the frog catching to Langfoot. She gave orders as if she had spent a couple of years at the military academy. Langfoot do this, and Langfoot do that. His face turned red and after a while he just lay down next to the anthill. She didn't say another word. It seemed to him she had been waiting for this. To come up with frog catching was not at all a dumb idea.

"Why did you come along, anyway? It's not part of your job, and I doubt whether the cook will be preparing any supper for you. And if I should happen to play the piano, it's certainly not so that you will crouch below the window and make dumb faces. What's your first name, anyway?"

"I'll only begin to give names after you get those restless legs of yours to quiet down some more."

"What makes you think you're so great? When you're someone for whom others are supposed to show respect, you don't spend your life in rags."

"People only think that way when they don't have the courage to be less than what they affect to be."

"Well bless my soul! You're starting to get your dander up."

"Not unless the wind coming from your direction raised it."

"Hang on there, friend! I could have made a mistake too when you get right down to it. Seriously though, what is really your name? I'm curious to know. As it happens, I've already thought up a cute first name for you."

"Not far removed from Schlemihl, I suppose."

"Peter, isn't it?"

"Johann Peter. Not Johann Wolfgang. There's a big difference between the two, you see. Indeed, it would have been very underhanded of my father to have Wolfgang inscribed in the church records in place of Peter."

"Why don't you stay earthbound, Peter? Allusions by themselves don't get me very excited."

"Then I have to ask you, what exactly is it you want from me?"

"Hold it, aren't you the one who wants something?"

"And you voluntarily walk into the trap? I must confess to you that with Henrietta I have all that's necessary to meet the occasional need. Come morning, I would even marry her – for a short time – if the boss were willing to pay me a decent day's wage. I'd like to request that you put in a good word for me with your father by the way."

"You keep making the situation more complicated."

"It's not my fault that there has to be so much beating around the bush."

"Is playing the piano also considered to be beating around the bush? Why don't you play it then?"

"I told you already, you must first exercise more control over those restless legs of yours."

"So why don't you hold my legs still if you're not pleased by such restlessness? Do you find my legs any uglier than others?"

"A decision on that requires time. I still have plenty of time to spare. Nothing is getting away from me. Unless it's my own self. Or do you honestly think that I'm content as a cow inside my own hide?"

"And yet you want to marry Henrietta?"

"The name doesn't matter. Nor does the face. Maybe not even the underpinnings, where people do their lovemaking. And certainly the duration of such love matters very little indeed."

"What does then?"

"It's what remains of it when it's over that matters. In a person's thoughts, I mean. In my thoughts and yours."

"I don't understand that."

"But you'd like to understand it. You're the curious type. It's your curiosity that keeps you from enjoying anything. You could just as easily flutter your eyelashes at the men in Paris or Berlin, not just here, where you risk hitting on one who doesn't understand a joke."

"Just why are you talking so much? There's no doubt you'd have gone a lot farther already if you weren't always thinking, and asking, and waiting for answers. Or do you really believe that the mask you've pulled over your face is not transparent?"

"That would make me angry."

With that he leaped through the air and gave her face a sharp upward twist. And he held her eyes and mouth still for an eternity. He was like an animal. He was panting in the gusty, humid penumbra of the rising twilight. And he lay before her body like a bush struggling tremulously against a strong wind. She had to pull him back up as one might pull a heavy net out of the water. She caressed his hair. His eyes were wide open. He had a very different face all of a sudden. It sent a shiver right through her. She felt as if she should be ashamed of something.

They fluttered across the fields as if two black strips of shadow had risen straight up.

"Tomorrow you'll be moving out, Peter. You'll be living at the gardener's place from now on. His living quarters are clean. If you like, I'll even have them put a stuffed chair in there. And as of now you'll concern yourself only with the plantation. I may even ride into the city this week too. You must wear clothes that are a little more civilized. You must also bury your nose in a book again so that you'll finally be rid of all those useless thoughts."

"What for, Paulina?"

"Because this vagabond role doesn't suit you anymore. You have long since outgrown the silly masquerade."

"It doesn't suit you anymore?"

"Suit *you*, I said, Peter!"

"Quite a few things don't suit me. And yet they have left me with indelible marks."

"It's all going to depend on how much of you can still be straightened back out. I have time. At least as much time as you do."

She gave him a hurried kiss and slipped across to the farm. He carried the bucket and the equipment into the kitchen and asked them to pour him a pitcher of milk. He downed it as if everything inside him were ripped and torn. When he went up to his straw bunk, Carlotta was lying in it. The long wait had tired her. She was sound asleep, and the moon illuminated her swollen face. Langfoot recoiled when he saw the open mouth ... and when he realized that it was Carlotta and not Henrietta. It gave him the shivers. For a long time he stood there, immovable. Inside his head the birds were making a commotion. He squatted down to rub the nagging pain in his knees. Carlotta's heavy breathing blended in with his. He was breathing faster. His body was completely at odds with itself. What was to happen next, and what had happened so far anyway?

He called Paulina to mind again. Her image stirred up a lot of memories. Many faces that resembled Paulina's. Many expectant moments like those on the banks of the lagoon. Only the vegetation had a different color. Only the roots had a different smell.

He couldn't straighten out his thoughts. The round window was turning red. Paulina's face evaporated into it. Henrietta's face took shape in it. Carlotta's face burned in it.

That's when he pulled his gunny sack out of the corner. The tin can rattled. Even the stairs managed to squeak while he crept down them. Once outside he headed directly into the rising sun. Heavy fog lay over the fields. He stomped through it. He was determined to reach one of the misty blue mountain ranges in the distance. In front of him the sun continued to rise, and at his back, driving full force, came the wind from the *estancia*.

Chapter Nine

By the time November came the voracious sun was already bearing down upon the rocky field so stubbornly and with such barbaric white-heat that even the legendary great-grandmothers of the Indians couldn't remember ever having experienced a hot spell like it, nor any that was even approximately that terrible. Not even in January and February, their hottest season. It was during these two months, which form the peak of summer on the upper course of the Paraná River, that by seeing their children grow into grandfathers and their great-grandchildren turn into muscular boys and graceful girls, people had acquired a practical notion of which heat is bearable versus which isn't.

But though the present year had behaved quite well until now, the fact that rice which had scarcely sprouted stalks was turning brown and no longer even promised a good yield in straw, that coffee blossoms were falling from their pistils like little piles of dirty yellow powder, that corn was burning up in the husk and sweet potatoes were actually forgetting to become tubers while still in the field, that the syrup in the sugarcane wasn't reaching liquid form, and that girls were only available for an embrace in the cool, moist twilight hours: this compounded the dreadful natural phenomenon that had spread over the landscape like the low-slung vault of some leaden baking oven. As an external force it made people seem tired, moody, and irritable, and inwardly they were upset; they became more sensitive to Biblical accounts of a God of wrath and vengeance. But what more could He avenge on a people so impoverished?

Yet as poor a hand as prosperity has dealt these people, nobody can endure a miserable life with any more patience than they can.

The only man within a ten mile radius whose outlook couldn't be spoiled by either the heat or the old women's whining was the man known to us as Johann Peter Langfoot. And what he minded perhaps least was the young girls' listlessness when it came to granting a token of their love.

Furthermore our friend Johann Peter Langfoot was also the only male in those parts who possessed a linen shirt. He pulled it out of his knapsack, rolled it out, slipped it on, and left it open at the chest so that the unruly curls of matted hair could be seen. In addition he whittled himself a handy walking stick out of a young *espinillo* and while doing so watched the buzzards crouch atop the bare branches of a *muermo* tree, looking like a bunch of rotting black pumpkins.

And because Johann Peter Langfoot's assistance wasn't needed to farm the *chacra* either, given that field work was the furthest thing from everyone's mind and that the people all lay sprawled out in their darkened mud huts, having no end of trouble with their bitter canned oranges (and not even daring to light up their pipes), Johann Peter would crisscross the fields, rest in the shade of a listless mimosa tree, catch himself a monkey that thirst had rendered quite tame, play with it for an hour or two, and finally allow it to leap back up where it felt at home.

In the marsh smothered turtles lay about with their sulfur-yellow, green and red-dotted abdomens exposed. In the cracks and crevices of the *barranca* the otherwise rarely visible coral snake could be seen sunning itself. The wildcat would quietly let the partridges amble by, ducking out of sight as soon as Langfoot came into view for fear that at any moment he might raise his club to strike it a blow.

But Langfoot was just pulling a thorn from the sole of his foot. Actually he had, with close to artistic virtuosity, raised his foot up to his lips and pulled out a black cactus needle using his teeth. That along with it he had simultaneously pulled out a piece of flesh was to him no cause for further concern.

Now he could stride along with his previous speed and agility, and he ended up over by the brickworks. There, for some unfathomable reason, they had allowed the furnace fires to go out. The mud bricks were cooking all by themselves laying out in the sun, and down in the pit the dirt in the hopper wagons looked as if it had been resting there undisturbed for at least a decade. The only way to remove it now would be to blast it out with a handful of gunpowder or a stick of dynamite. Four weeks more and the stuff would be completely turned to stone, thereby becoming a new mineral deposit in the soil below. The Slovak brickmakers had fled into the villages and lay stark naked on the bare stone floors of the houses.

The women and girls who went in and out didn't even view that as anything objectionable although at other times they blushed well above their ears when a man came out of the water in broad daylight wearing only bathing trunks.

Up near the rookery stood the pathetic looking shack owned by the watchman at *Estancia Santa Juana*. There was just one room in his entire proletarian palace. A hole in the wall where a person slept, cooked, and celebrated his birthdays. A place where you could throw yourself onto the corn straw and stretch out when the time came to die. It was also the place where, out of the same straw, you lifted your newborn child. Until now the children here had all been girls; the watchman already had seven of them, and the eighth was on the way. Ironically the man was already as gray around the temples as the torn bark of the three eucalyptus trees in front of his hut.

Langfoot found the entire company in the shade of the three old trees; they were sucking on the *bombillas* of their *mate* gourds, and the head of the house was surveying the harvest of his lust much as God in heaven had once looked out over the world he created as it lay before his laughing, satisfied, brown eyes. Admittedly, it's not certain yet whether the God we hold dear has brown or blue eyes, but those of the watchman are tobacco brown. And on top of that the man is a dyed-in-the-wool native *criollo*.

There were just two slits under his eyebrows through which something dark and shiny flashed as the man sat there smugly grinning at that lout Langfoot for sheer satisfaction over the fruitfulness of his family. The beard alone made it impossible to tell where his mouth was and on his trousers were patches in at least forty different shades.

Langfoot joined the group for a good hour. Indeed, the watchman's wife turned her back on him for fear of looking 'indiscreetly' at the monkeyman with the shaggy chest of hair. Particularly since she wasn't yet sure whether the eighth child, which was already merrily bouncing around in her belly, was going to be a boy or a girl.

It was Langfoot's opinion that it was bound to be a daughter this time. Naturally he only said this to irritate the watchman, who finally wanted to have a boy and had sworn to himself that he would not quit making children until the boy was really there.

Of course Langfoot was more interested in girls – other men's naturally – of the kind that's already grown up and pleasantly fattened.

He stroked the sunken cheeks of the watchman's eldest daughter and quickly told another story about Devil Ram and the Rye Scarecrow as if this child had grown up between Bromberg and Pillkallen and been raised on German slop. It was simply in his nature to use low key insanity in order to frighten people like these, who could neither write nor read a printed word. And the stupid girl was listening as if it would satisfy her hunger.

After that visit with the watchman's family Langfoot jaunted back across the parched fields. Never had he seen such puny peanut plants around this time of year. He also searched the skies in vain for the sign of any bird. Not even the crickets interrupted the tranquility with their fiddling. It was at the crossing, however, that the Indian Itatubo met up with him by the rock that served as a kind of arrow pointing travelers to the city of Corrientes; he wanted at all costs to foist upon Langfoot a pretty, yellow lemon that was fairly bursting with acidity. Right away you want twenty *centavos* for a lemon like that? Be on about your business, you old bowlegged pagan!

But he showed him the way to the *estancia* anyway. There was not one tree or bush anywhere on that stretch. The sun had passed high noon long ago. It might be to the Indian's advantage that the people on the ranch were all much too tired and worn out to even imagine what a lemon looked like.

When Langfoot had already reached the heights and the citrus vendor was lying on the side of the road pressing one lemon after another on his parched lips, it occurred to Langfoot that it was about time for him to look up a person named Vicente Ujacha, who was supposed to be stranded here. In the village people simply called him 'Jach.' He himself preferred to hear the shortened form of his name. Anything unduly long disgusted him to the depths of the dark soul that he happened to possess. That was also why he had never been able to keep his *pesos* together. In his opinion life was already complicated enough, and they simply made money too round; it ought to be rectangular with spikes. Life therefore was something he also chose to shorten with the help of a sparkling schnapps that he cooked up for himself using sugarcane, the juice of wild pineapples, seven different herbs, and some pepper pods. He could have been a commercial success with the skill he had for cooking up schnapps. But he abhorred business of every kind because people always insisted on haggling over the price. Also because he himself had an unquenchable thirst. So every week for the three days approximately that he spent downing liquor, soaking it up from top to bottom and stem to stern, he needed the next four to sleep off the effects of his binge. In this manner he had successfully drunk and slept away his farm, the warehouse, the *hierba* mill, and finally his own family. He had once spent a couple of weeks in town sleeping at the same boarding house as Langfoot. Ever since that time they had been friends. And each of them had his share of loons fluttering around in his head.

On stepping into Jach's half-collapsed wooden cabin, all that Langfoot could see on a messy bed made of reeds was a bundle of steaming, snoring flesh. But he also found the hole in the ground where the old drunk had hidden his schnapps. No sooner had Langfoot done that than he raised up the clay jug, took a good slug, maybe even three or four, and poured the rest out into the sun. He had in fact convinced himself that the merciless blazing heat would be overcome by that amount of alcohol and call in the rain to cool things off. Like it or not, malice was one of his greatest weaknesses. He had always reserved whatever was best for himself. Beyond that, let just a faint glimmer fall to the girls.

Making his way back up the heights again, he would probably have sighted the Paraná down below alongside the big city sometime that evening, but he was saddened by the plight of so many fields burned to ashes. All the walking on hot rocks had put blisters on his feet. Blue horseflies were buzzing around his head, attracted by the big drops of sweat that were dripping down from his temples and coming to a stop on his bare shoulders, leaving bright scarlet stains behind.

It's really quite insane, thought Langfoot, to knock down half a liter of schnapps in this stifling tropical heat. Still less understandable is Nature's mad refusal to spare the life of even a single stalk of grass or a single tree frog. Her denial of a cool gust of the wind to the treetops. And her withholding of a harvest from sharecroppers who had devoted months of effort and hard work to it. Nature was, in fact, swindling them in broad daylight for the whole world to see. Sheer madness. A dimwitted feat that would yet cause several generations of scientists to rack their brains uselessly before they became as smart as J.P. Morgan and as wise as the fakir who sits naked in the blazing sun twiddling his thumbs on a stomach shrunken by hunger while he draws nearer to the kingdom of heaven.

Langfoot had long since given up on his plans for becoming an itinerant lecturer. It would be easier to change stones into bread than to make these people understand that they were still stuck light years behind the times. But for the moment that was not what Langfoot had on his mind as he searched the heavens for a cloud. It was not a cloud that met his gaze but rather a wind sensor that had been erected up there by some unidentified agency. Smack in the middle of a field of clover, just where a person might otherwise stretch out in comfort and watch the white netting of the clouds. Of the clover only a rolling wave of frizzled, brown piles of weeds remained. At the very top amid the four vanes of the wind sensor an owl has nested as if no other more sinister, dilapidated ruin were to be found near or far. And if you put your ear to the wooden struts, you can distinctly hear the worm that has never experienced such relentless sunshine with its own eyes. And if you keep your ear up there a little while longer, such is the sound of rushing and flowing that the listener becomes convinced that the rain has also crawled into the wood with the wood worms and is now allowing its streams of gray water to gush around in there. Or could it perhaps be the Paraná below ground always in motion and which, after encountering an obstacle abandoned here by life itself, is simply forced to dry up like the sap of the spurge plant when its pedicel is broken off and the white, poisonous slime instantly petrifies into a stonelike drop that eats away the skin?

Langfoot journeyed across the singed black land for another three days and three nights before he saw the wide course of the Paraná stretching out below him. All of a sudden the thought had struck him not to return to the village. He had made no commitments that bound him to stay. The only things he was leaving behind were the smell of his useless poverty and the smile that people often had in their eyes when he'd tell them about all those colorful birds that had taken up residence inside his head, ... that demanded he feed them, ... that complicated his life.

He had made seven circles around the center of himself. Not one spot on either foot was free of injury. His face looked like tanned, brown leather. The walking stick had to stand in for one leg or the other in quick succession. Even his shirt was no longer white but yellow like the mud on the fields and hard like the parched weeds.

No longer being set in motion by the leaves, the trees had long since become irritating to him. He found a *ñandú* dead in a furrow of corn. With no water in them, ditches had lost their entire purpose. Only the red tile roof of a small church sparkled uninterruptedly. It enticed those who were still alive down towards the dead. Nor did it make any special effort to show its shriveled face in the mirror of the river anymore. It slept right along blurrily below the surface. It had no height and no depth.

Johann Peter Langfoot lay atop a cliff on the river's steep bank. He saw the thick smoke above the chimneys of the city. He could hear the commotion made by the cranes in the port. He could taste work on the outermost tip of his tongue, and he spit it out quickly in disgust. He felt as if the schnapps he had guzzled like water three days before had turned to bile inside his emotions.

He continued to wait for a fisherman to spread his sail. But no matter how hard you looked, there wasn't a boat to be seen the length and breadth of the river. Even now he still could not detect the least sign of a real cloud. He let his legs dangle straight down and thought of the frogs' hollow song in the rushes and tall reeds. These were the reeds from which he would cut the pan pipes. Another thing that came back to him was the melody that he used to play, half angry and half bemused, when the girls from the *chacra* would walk past the fence and strain their eyes to see the flute player. Many of these naive young things had lain with him hoping that such love could last forever. None had been promised more than he could fulfill. In his mind, life on the move fulfilled a greater purpose. He liked to say, "Good bye!"

In the end he was at a loss as to what else he might attempt – given his weathered skin and arrested thoughts – beyond jumping head first into the river below. The cliff rose about fifty feet out of the water. And he jumped off as surely and elegantly as if all his life he had done nothing else. When Langfoot emerged from the water, the river cast a wave all the way to the opposite bank for the first time in twenty-nine tedious days. And he could see where a small black cloud was rolling in from the west and would soon be rescuing the land and the river and the fields and all the creatures from the stifling heat. In less than fifteen minutes the driving rain would hit.

No one came and shook his hand for conjuring up the rain with that beautiful headlong dive of his. A policeman did come along, however, and wrote down his name for swimming at a spot where it was prohibited. It certainly wasn't Langfoot's fault that this worthy guardian of the peace, this pockmarked Indian native, couldn't understand the name and therefore took along the whole individual instead.

Chapter Ten

For five weeks now the rain had been pouring down without interruption. The lagoons were spilling over. The river that scarcely measured a few meters across in the summer raced through the decimated forest frothing like a storm-churned lake. The palm trees were bent right down to the surface of the waters. Drifting along in this maelstrom were severed treetops, thatched roofs, dead animals, and a Virgin Mary layered in gold. The white vultures were hacking themselves into a state of exhaustion. Some herons circled uneasily. Passing through the rapids, islands of vegetation turned in circles like tops never to stand still again until they reached the delta.

It was from the Andes that Langfoot had come, down from Jujuy. He had worked for a few weeks in the tanning factories. His face was stained reddish brown by the caustic solutions in the primitive steeping kettles.

Already tufts of gray were springing up amid the still plentiful hair of his temples.

It wasn't so much the tannic acid that had brought Langfoot down; if the truth be known, he had come down for the feeder cattle. He was the one herding them into the cattle cars out in the vast stockyard. Day after day, five hundred, six hundred, eight hundred head. Shorthorn, Hereford and Angus. Yorkshire and East Friesian, Allgäu and Swiss. Black and white spotted steers. Slate gray steers. Fiery red steers. Steers pale as the moon. Steers with twisted horns; steers with almost perfectly straight horns growing out sideways. Steers with no horns at all. Steers whose noses had to be ripped half open with pincers before they'd do you the favor of moving two or three feet. Steers that would eat out of your hand. And another strain that wouldn't think twice about picking a man up on their horns as if he were just one of the many playthings toyed with daily out in the lush pasture land.

Langfoot thought to himself: If I, who certainly was not born to the trade, go on doing work like this for a few more weeks, chances are good that my esteemed colleagues might mistake me for the dumbest steer of the lot and herd me into the cattle car. Nothing will remind a man of his own spotty animal skin sooner than daily interaction with cattle that have been matured for the slaughterhouses. I would truly like to know what difference there is between a carload of cattle headed for slaughter and a carload of soldiers being shipped from East to West and from West back East to be slaughtered on the battlefields. For by his standards the steer is also dying a death he certainly was not looking forward to. On the contrary to avoid it he beats a wide path around it. This is a death he can sniff at a distance of one hundred miles, so he speeds off across the pampas in a terrified effort to escape the hideous smell that exudes from the cattle cars. He hardly notices when thirst hunkers down in his bloodshot eye sockets and beats on his flanks with a club. He endures it as if it were only the insect bite of some horsefly, the kind one flick of the tail will rid you of in times when the great drought has burned the grass right down to the last fibers of its roots. He suffers hunger and thirst with a bilious wrath seething inside him. But his knees go soft when the shrill whistle of the locomotive reminds him that he is now ready for the long-bladed knife.

This was something Johann Peter Langfoot simply couldn't stand by and watch any more. He could see that the Indians and the Creoles, and even his own compatriots, didn't give a hoot about what steers like that feel when someone slashes open their side with a steel hook. It didn't matter that of twenty animals they might round up initially there would only be twelve left whose lungs were not so badly scorched that they could still march through the narrow door to receive the blow of the hammer, the last torture stop before the knife. That's just how it is down where people are as compulsive about killing steers as they are about drinking *mate* or putting children into the world.

What have I to do with this barbaric slaughter of living beings? he wondered. Doing this a fellow can hardly earn enough to satisfy his hunger and is only able visit the cathouse once every three or four weeks at best. There's even less to spare for cigars, and he's only allowed to taste the *caña* up front on the tip of his tongue instead of chugging so much of it that his guts turn inside out. Still the locals get their money's worth for riding the herd. For them it is satisfaction enough if they can hang a thick brass chain over their bellies, tie a white scarf around their necks, and stand around in front of a movie theater telling each other raunchy jokes.

But where are the sun and the soft island of grass in which to stretch out when summer comes tumbling down rich with nuts? When the poppies are dripping red in the wheat fields and the green throated sparrow hawk is circling high above … the length of the Paraná's broad waters? Summer was there, but only for the better souls. It was there: down in the orchid woods; among the knotty shafts of the palm trees; under the *quebracho* tree; under the magnolia; on the river banks; amid the stilted pink flamingos; among the river dolphins; amidst the chattering monkeys and the bluetailed *aras*; down in the myrtle grove; in the perfume of the daffodils, the sage, the oleander. Summer also brought the bite of a Quechua woman on the nape of Langfoot's neck; from a woman as supple as the tendril of a vine. Her hair weighed heavily in the cups of one's hands, and her mouth was filled with lust.

But here beneath the first outcroppings of the Cordillera there were hills and valleys meandering as closely by as in Europe. What agony it is still to keep wanting to fashion myself a cheerful existence out of the last sighs of my self! Merely to keep from sinking into depravity. To keep from turning scabrous. To avoid exploding into a cloud of smelly fumes like an overgrown potato. Always masquerading. Always the Schlemihl. Another Ahasverus. Nowhere to call home and nowhere to go. Even less so than the alligator whose jaws are forced open by the wood of the trap. Even less so than a moth that is first lulled by ether before having a needle bore through his body … so that once embalmed, it may demonstrate the unimaginable wonders of nature under the glass of a display case. And finally still less so than that *yerba* grass which is chopped down so that it can be sipped out of a silver-rimmed gourd in the form of a medicinal tea and be ranked "most sacred product of the nation."

But here among the purple thistles and fuchsia shrubs, among the bell flowers and tulip trees, there shivers a human wreck. It is the final degradation of what is discernibly still a male countenance in panicky, stygian fright. Everything is clamoring. Everything is spreading. Everything is streaming forth. And there seems to be no end to the din of the perpetually receding and always fleeing steps of neither here nor there. Human kind. But what kind of being is this anyway?

Johann Peter Langfoot painfully shuffled along farther and farther still, tattered in mind and body, his hair matted from his lengthy journeys. His feet were covered with blisters from the eternal resistance of the miles. He was on the southbound highway passing by streams. His shoes were drawing water. The wind was nestling into the greasy, sun-bleached coat he wore with its green rain stains, and it was feeding on the warmth emanating from his body, because inside his blood was boiling with a worthless fever.

Occasionally his path would lead him to a *rancho*. Occasionally he would take heart in hand and walk up to the barbed wire fence. Then he'd clap his hands though he had little to sell; his skill as a handyman was about all. But that wasn't needed here. That was even cheaper here. Yet the only thing left in his belly was wind. He looked at the children, who lay out in the sun just as their mother's womb had delivered them, dirty and steaming. They lay in a sea of dock weeds and had nothing to chew. The water in the cisterns tasted as foul as the muck of the goats. Not one mortal soul could refer him to a job to save his life. *Paciencia*, old friend. In four weeks the corn will have reached the point where we can hack it down.

An Indian woman that Johann Peter Langfoot eventually met at the crossroads while they were harvesting herbs there said this to him because he had helped her pull chamomile and horsetail out of the overgrown soil: "There is a lot of work to be found in this country. You just have to know how to pick it up. Keep going down this creek, way on down, until it gets so wide that a horse can no longer jump it. Then go on for another piece until the point where people are already taking a boat across from one bank to the other. And where it's finally real wide and crashes off some cliffs into another stream ... that's where I think you'll find work in the rice fields. That's where I think my daughter probably still has a job. Tell her that you ran into me. Her name is Naranja. And if by now the child in her belly should be ripe, then she should come back here and help me with the herbs. They're back up to paying half a *peso* for a kilogram of horsetail now if it's been neatly sorted and dried. Next month the pigweed will also be ripe, and I'll probably have to lie with my son-in-law because Malva hasn't put one in the oven yet. At least one of us should have one in the oven, or else the family will get a bad reputation...."

"But it could just as well be your son-in-law's problem," said Langfoot with a grin to the woman.

"You'll be back after the sugar harvest, and then we'll see who's right and whether you're a better son-in-law."

"It's a deal, grandma!" replied Langfoot as he tried to give the old woman a kiss on the cheek, right where her plug of coca leaves was inserted. But this proved to be just one more instance of his avian thoughts misfiring. Because the old woman whacked him across the fingers with her cutting blade and shouted that he should never show his face there again. There was, after all, no need for swine of that sort.

Johann Peter Langfoot took to his heels and headed off. Reflecting on what the old battle-axe had paid him for his help, he said to himself: If your daughter has descended from the same tree as you have, I'd just as soon someone else take the rice fields.

At the fork in the road he stumbled upon an orange tree that had matured in the wild and plucked himself some of its ripe fruit. He stuffed so much of it down that he couldn't even move his extremities. Inside his mouth, his tongue felt as if the top seven layers of skin had been removed by a steel grater. He spent the night under the tree as well. Come morning his legs were as stiff as a withered pair of acacia limbs. After weeks of steady rain, the sun was still being very stingy with its warmth. Due to the tremendous level of humidity, the air was as thick as jam made of unripe pineapples.

The rice fields were out of the picture for good now. Instead at a bend in the stream a primitive sawmill came into view. Truly a ramshackle affair. Something out of the nineteenth century. The boss was a Norwegian who had jumped ship many years back. Thirty years had already gone by since both he and his brother had deserted. Now he was at least pushing seventy, and the 'chalet' made of bare boards in which he lived was hardly any younger.

"Of course there are a couple of weeks work to be had here, you oaf!" he said to Johann Peter Langfoot. "You'll find proper work with me, all right. This is where you'll need to put your shoulder firmly to the grindstone and not immediately fall face down in the muck. How long have you been knocking around like this, anyway? Do you want to give it a whirl, or not? The one thing I can't give you, though, is wages. But on the whole at my place you should eat your fill. That's something you appear to need urgently. A cucumber could certainly not look any greener. That can't possibly come from enjoying too much meat."

Johann Peter Langfoot grinned and allowed himself some private thoughts. After stowing his travel bag under a pile of boards, the next thing he did was sit down at the table. The boss's remarks about good food had been no exaggeration. What was placed in front of Johann Peter Langfoot was an authentic *puchero*. It's amazing what that can accomplish when the meat hasn't come from a hundred year old billy goat, when the kernels of corn are not sugary, the cabbage is not swimming in gunk, and the sweet potatoes aren't rotten. It's likely to make the lame see again and put the blind back on their feet. Langfoot chewed until his jawbones started to pop. And the boss stood right next to him and laughed until the tears rolled down his cheeks. In the excitement he forgot to have his own lunch. There wasn't anything left over for him anyway. Langfoot didn't have to be asked twice either. And to conclude this repast there was sugarcane schnapps – the real, green, spicy kind.

As beginnings go this was turning out splendidly, thought Langfoot to himself. The coloration of his face slowly returned to something reasonably human. And when the boss asked him if he had no other trousers to put on beyond his frayed stovepipes, Langfoot grumbled, "When the harvest turns out as badly as it has this year, you can't ask God to supply breeches of English cowhide for the kind of drudgery that's done in a sawmill."

"So that's the cloth you're cut from, eh?" answered the boss. "Just hold your horses, maybe a fresh set of clothes will turn up for you here at my place. But you'll have to put all you've got to the task, just like you did earlier with that *puchero* of which you didn't even leave me enough for toothpicks. If you just take half the workload off my hands, then a solid and lasting friendship is bound to develop between us."

The days that followed were filled with strenuous labor. At first Langfoot could never carry more than four boards down to the shed. Later on he worked his way up to six and seven. In the process his face gradually brightened up. Ultimately his eyes began to twinkle as if he were polishing them every morning with agate.

"Well, well ... , you have now reached the stage where you can be seen among men again," said the boss after four weeks had passed. And he took Johann Peter along to see his brother Laase. Laase owned a small *boliche*, or tavern, in the fishing village that lay about an hour's distance from there. Laase was also the only European among the ten fishermen who lived in Tacahua. The others were all still dyed-in-the-wool Indians. Langfoot could not understand the mumbo jumbo they spoke. It wasn't really a mumbo jumbo either; instead it was a mumbo Guaraní. For him the boss had to interpret it first into mumbo Spanish. Strange people, these Indian fishermen, thought Langfoot. I'd sure like to know just where their voice is situated; is it in the stomach or in the back of their head? I mean, you get a better tune from a child's tin horn that's been run over by a car than you do from them. But they can sure drink with the best of them.

One thing was certain: *señor* Laase, or don Enrique as he had the local people call him, had an excellent business relationship with them. In addition to serving finer beverages he also had a general store. There you could find chocolate and matches, neckerchiefs and bush knives, calico and kerosene, lipstick and peppermint tea. There were bracelets for the women and silver spurs for the cowboys who visited the village every now and then. On the high and holy *Reconquista* days they even held a huge gala picture show.

Johann Peter Langfoot now went over to don Enrique's place every Sunday. The boss gladly paid for whatever he drank and smoked. In return he had to play Laase's accordion. The wives and children of the fishermen would stick their unkempt faces through the window. They weren't allowed into the taproom; it was forbidden by the *gobernación*. And Laase didn't want that raw nerve exposed anyway. The men were already carrying their knives loosely enough as it was.

Sometimes Langfoot also let the boss tramp over to Tacahua alone. That always happened when Langfoot was being tormented by his thoughts. He couldn't escape them. They kept coming back. And he couldn't get the birds in his head to settle down either. Time had made them older but certainly no less quarrelsome.

He lay on the hill beyond the sawmill. Bending in the wind nearby were some magnificent aspen trees. The parrots were putting on a raucous show. Intermittently you could hear the song of a small gray bird like a thrush. Langfoot was twirling his thumbs. Nothing else came to mind but those other, weightier thoughts. He glanced over at the sawmill. Clinging to the vegetation on the riverbank like a bird's nest and resembling a dwarf in size, it stared with its paneless windows across a body of water that was turning into a reservoir thanks to a dam built of stacked tree trunks. The existence of the sawmill owner was like another Robinson Crusoe story. Here was the ultimate hideaway for people who had brought their worldly affairs to an end.

Langfoot thought: The boss man could certainly spare me some dough. I deserve at least a *peso* a day for the work I'm putting in. I have fifty-nine days worth of work behind me now. That's enough to restore a sensible weight to my chest pouch again.

He resolved to give the old man a suitably sharp nudge in the ribs as soon as he came back from boozing it up. Compounding the matter were those leather breeches from England that the boss had promised him and which had supposedly been on their way for quite some time now. However what no one could have suspected, least of all Langfoot, was that the old man should be felled by a stroke at the very moment in which he meant to raise his last glass....

The sawmill belonged to Eric Laase now. The justice of the peace still had to issue all the proper documents and seals. Until then not a single wheel was allowed to turn.

"But you can stay if you're inclined to and if the work is still to your taste," said Laase to Langfoot. "I just can't pay you any wages in the meantime. You're a widely traveled man, even an educated man according to what my brother said. It seems to me you should know what reason dictates in a case like ours."

"Fair enough!" answered Langfoot. "But you should pay me the wages I'm due for fifty-nine days of work. Or am I supposed to wait until the justice of the peace has spoken his mind?"

"What's this ... , are you actually showing yourself to be a scrapper like that right before my eyes? You intend to demand your salary twice over? Well, listen here, my grandfather was not a man to owe debts, and my brother even less so. He'd usually pay his debts beforehand ... most of the time. How unpleasant it was for him to discover that a farmer had sold him lumber too cheaply. No, my friend! My brother even paid for his coffin ahead of time of course. And here you are pretending that he didn't pay you subsequently what you hadn't even earned! You're an absolute scoundrel! I don't even want to smell your shadow three hours from now."

"You've revealed yourself to be what I had never taken you for," said Langfoot. "As of now, of course, you and I are finished. But I'll still throw a pine branch on the old man's grave. At least he always gave me my fill to eat. You on the other hand would add up every single bite I consumed, wouldn't you? You can have the fifty-nine *pesos*. After you incubate them, stinking piles of manure will crawl out from underneath. You may eventually need them again to fill your stomach. But the Devil can take you for all I care!"

Johann Peter Langfoot was unable to find even one scrap of his canvas bag. The rats under the woodpile had done a thorough job of it. Their young were squeaking inside the tin can.

Oh well, said Langfoot to himself. There isn't even anything to gain by crossing myself three times behind this dump! And there's equally little to gain by looking back at the waterfalls. That's sure not where my fifty-nine *pesos* will be surfacing.

As for you, old man, I hope the worms don't dig into your body all too forcefully. May they do a clean job on the flesh and bones. It'll be some time before anyone gets to taste another dandy *puchero* like yours.

I'll just have to owe you the pine branch for a while longer. I've noticed the stuff doesn't grow around here. For now then, "*Adiós.*"

By the time he had gotten his breath back and became aware of the raunchy smell that emanated from his person, immense fields of corn were stretching out on either side of the road. A young mother sat in the clearing that stretched around an ancient magnolia tree and offered her naked breast to her wriggling infant.

This might eventually bring me luck, whispered Langfoot to himself, and addressed the young mother with even greater friendliness than that with which one here customarily greets clergymen who are still young and handsome. Young and handsome … , the description was uncannily appropriate for the young madonna who was huddling here by the path. And she even allowed Johann to caress her hair. As he caressed it, strangely unsettling vibrations traveled through his hands.

Chapter Eleven

"Look here now, man, don't go on telling me so much about God. For the moment it's the locusts who still determine whether anyone is going to have a good harvest or whether he can pack his bundle again. Things are set up so that the hobos don't die out in this promised land. It's been eight days since anything warm has trickled down my throat. Give me a dark corner where I can stretch out and a pelt, so my skull doesn't develop any lumps. Whatever tastes good to you would have been more than tasty for me. Only I can perhaps raise my spoon to my lips faster than you can."

These were the words of Johann Peter Langfoot to Hein Schäffers as he sat crouched before his *rancho* gazing worriedly over the new crop of potatoes that was being choked by weeds. A dry branch fell off the eucalyptus tree that stood in front of the rundown wooden shack, and Hein Schäffers answered: "But I can't pay you anything. At least not at the beginning. At this point I must consider myself lucky if the storekeeper lets me put salt on account. Do write down where you'll be staying though. And after I've safely taken the harvest to town, I will, of course, send you some money. No one has that bit of surplus muscle fat to give away anymore. Not that working your fingers down to the bone is worth a hill of beans nowadays. Even what a bird drops on your head has its own significance. Be happy that you didn't hit on the worthless idea of acquiring your own farmstead. As a matter of fact I would also have done better and stayed healthier if I had remained in the coal pits of the Ruhr. The dues I have had to pay here in apprenticeship will be enjoyed by the next generation. And I don't even know if or when I can ever bring my family over to join me."

He shoved the straw on which he was chewing over to the other corner of his mouth. The bitterness of this land lay beneath his tongue. He turned to spit, but that was not enough with which to push aside a life of misery, for he had still not assimilated the quiet wisdom of the Indians.

And only after another long while did Johann Peter Langfoot respond: "Why are you echoing everything I say, you fool! Just a while ago, you still looked forward to the Good Lord and to a *hacienda* with a natural well in front of your veranda. With white pebble paths under your belly and a cigar in your snout.

"As you can see, the birds in my brain are momentarily behaving themselves and keeping quiet. Let me get busy with the weeds. I'll roll a cartload of stones up from the pit. I'll draw the furrows for the grapevines. We'll dig the holes for the olive trees. I have long since broken the habit of having blisters on my hands. Nor can sweat be pressed from my skin anymore. But if you played a tune or two on your accordion every evening, I might even sing along. Do you by chance have a superior bottle of sugarcane brandy at the house? Otherwise I'd have to trek all the way back to that general store just to wet my whistle and then watch the *almacenero* chalk up my God blessed paycheck for it. You don't need to pay that man an employment fee either, because he sent me over to your neighbor on the right. And if your neighbor hadn't just finished whipping the tar out of one of his little boys, you'd be looking out for those weeds of yours by yourself. I just can't bear to see children crying. And where there are children crying in a home, the Devil is sure to be sitting up on the roof having himself a good laugh. Don't forget that bottle of *caña* for me though. And another thing, show me how a person who's aiming at a varmint can always manage to spit beside it."

"Why not? You are to have a bottle of the only authentic *caña* there is, from Paraguay. Perhaps we'll polish it off some evening after I have first convinced myself that your fists work as vigorously as your jawbone just did. Hell's bells, don't do that again!"

He went into the house and returned with an earthenware pitcher and a piece of bread. He had a nose that had been flattened as if he had once been a boxer. The ears didn't fit though. And the heavy field work had already taken quite a toll on his back. In his gray-blue eyes however shone the endless expanse of this land with a light, sulfury shimmer.

He offered the jug to Johann Peter Langfoot: "Well, have yourself a big swig then. And if your teeth are not too black, you can give the bread a try too. Fresh bread is only available every eight days. Ohle Hansen bakes mine along with his. But usually by Wednesday it's gone."

Johann Peter Langfoot duly took a big slug of the smooth-tasting *caña*. He'd gladly have taken a second one too. He just didn't want himself looking like a drunkard right from day one. He bit into the bread. The smacking of his lips made the grasses start undulating. There were butterflies darting up and around the roof. An armadillo rolled itself into a ball in the wild camellia bushes. And Hein Schäffers did his part by playing a piece on the accordion. In the meantime the moon had also risen; it was shaped like a very slender sickle and lay on its belly. The mosquitos came swarming out. Bats were thumping up against the house, and the big green fireflies were flickering out among the potatoes. On the hill a herd of sheep ambled by as if the clouds were tired of the sky and wanted to give the earth a try for a change.

All of a sudden Hein Schäffers broke off what he was playing on the accordion. Johann Peter Langfoot glanced over in his direction. He shrugged his shoulders. Finally he said, "On serious reflection, I really ought to be properly whipped."

"Yes, well … , my dear Hein, the thistles back in Bochum have their own share of thorns. But whether you sell your soul for a pint of pale beer or for a *caña*, it all boils down to the same thing. Go on, have a slug with me. Tomorrow I'll also tell you something to make you laugh."

They both took a healthy swig from the clay jug. And Langfoot wiped his mouth with the back of his hand. Hein finished playing the rest of his tune. The clouds had clambered back up into the sky. And in the twilight standing there quite aimlessly in the middle of the field was a tree.

"All right," said Johann Peter Langfoot finally, "we have a contract. However long it's meant to last will not depend on the two of us. And now I would like to stretch out."

That was his debut with Hein Schäffers in the Terrabussa colony two hundred kilometers south of San Juan. Within four weeks each of the eighteen local German colonists could tell a separate quaint anecdote about Johann Peter Langfoot. He was simply the man he was. And that was precisely what seemed quite outlandish and crazy, even to these poor people who had long since forgotten the meaning of fun.

From five o'clock in the morning until sometime between eleven and noon Johann Peter Langfoot lay in the potato field contending with thistles. What's more, possibly the sharpest of all were the ever protruding bromeliads, including horsetail, pineapple tendrils, yarrow, and spurge. He had made himself a pair of knee pads by wrapping lambskin around his joints and was carefully hacking around each potato plant with his bush knife. He could not pull out the weeds, or the still tender roots of the tubers would have come up with them. Two hours or so in the midday sun would quickly have sufficed to turn their green into black.

This special weeding technique was something in which Hein Schäffers had not needed to give him a lot of training. He went about his task as if he had already spent years working with a crew on a sweet potato farm. He knew some tricks that not even Hein Schäffers was familiar with. And for him this was the third planting season experienced here as a colonist. Next year he was thinking of putting in a crop of beans. The canning factory in San Juan would take any quantity off his hands. And with each successive year he intended to expand his vineyard. Ultimately the entire area to which he was entitled was to be planted with grapes. All the Terrabussa colonists hoped to rake in a fortune with wine. The first million *pesos*, that was everyone's dream. For the sake of this crazy dream they threw themselves into harness for up to five or six years, allowed the very marrow in their bones to dry up, lived like animals while tilling soil that had once borne wheat and corn but had then lain fallow for a decade; one step after another, one level at a time, all for the unbending rows of the vine.

But two failed harvests in quick succession – the first in his second year and another in the third – and suddenly that beautiful dream of God's vineyard in the San Juan hinterland hinged on little more than a walking stick. On the other hand capital placed in tracts of land merely for safekeeping was making those investors fat who left their acreage untilled. The procedure was comparable to that of warehousing lumber or putting cowhide in storage until the next rise on the world commodities markets.

Within five weeks the potato field was clean although there were again thistles as tall as a man where they had begun their work five weeks earlier; beneath, however, the potato plants had doubled in height and were not so easily cheated of fresh air by the horsetail and rue. Partridges gobbled their way about the furrows. They didn't do much damage. Johann Peter Langfoot was skillful at catching them with snares made of hemp and for three weeks they enjoyed a change of fare by eating roast partridge every night. Fancy preparation was of no concern. They often gulped everything down with a hearty appetite, including the entrails and half of the feathers. Their stomachs were intent on nourishment and digested it all.

The skin on Langfoot's face had already turned leathery twice. He would see it happen five more times before the summer was over. And if by Michaelmas the locusts hadn't radically chewed away most of the crop, then the people might safely speak of a good harvest. Langfoot decided to go ahead and wait for that decisive day to roll around, even though Hein Schäffers had run out of fresh accordion pieces. In the meanwhile it was his neighbor Hellweg who had popped over one evening and given the squeeze box a workout. He was originally from around Hanover, and there was still something of the Lüneburg heath about him. What he played was as dry as the gorse on a broomstick in winter. But his vineyard was complete, plus he had seven sons and a pockmarked Indian for a wife. From this lowly loyal soul, however, had sprung only one son. The boy didn't look like an Indian and not like the Lüneburg heath either. More like a large specimen from the Ivory Coast; he had a head full of woolly hair and a nose as wide across as his entire face.

"It's a good thing I'm not a young, white, pregnant girl," said Johann Peter Langfoot, "people might otherwise get the wrong impression." And he took Christian Hellweg's black son up onto his lap and sang him the beautiful ballad of the bandit Rinaldo Rinaldini. And the Indian woman stood alongside scratching the top of her head in a thoughtful, even expressive, manner.

When Michaelmas came the whole colony lay smashed in the grass. The south wind had driven the swarms of locusts to Paraguay and Brazil. The brown jumpers stood nearly ten feet deep on the *yerba* fields of Iguaçú and Apiahy. And in Asunción the prices for *caña* and *mate* were rising. But to keep a steady price for coffee on the world markets, farmers had to shovel their beans under their cauldrons or else bake bricks with them. This year on the *yerba* fields it was the good Lord and his locusts who controlled the perpetually fluctuating ratio of supply and demand. This year in fact there was nothing to supply.

All of this was going through Johann Peter Langfoot's mind as he watched the people's drunkenness. The herons in the lagoon were making a hellish racket. Hein Schäffers lay in the reeds with his Indian mate wanting to know how the pieces fit together for the black youngster. Christian Hellweg accompanied them on the accordion. And Anton Gruber was heading back to the store for a fresh supply of *caña*. There would also be some sweets and a tin of anchovies. And when Langfoot asked Schäffers how it was down in the reeds among the black heron feathers, he answered, "Fair to middlin, old man. God only knows, we certainly aren't spoiled out in these parts."

The locusts had laid their eggs in Paraguay and around the Amazon. It was only for that reason that the crops here still stood tall and straight as soldiers. Hein Schäffers had been spared but then so had Jochen Peltzer, Hugo Schmidt, and Anton Diegele. This fall they would each be able to put in around a thousand additional grape cuttings. With time the potato crop, which is meant to ready the soil for the vine, would become more and more scarce. And what farmer would still hanker to waste his time on *maní* after that? Beans are what go into the furrows of the grape shoots. String free wax beans for the canning factory in San Juan. All of Argentina will be supplied with stringless wax beans from San Juan. And the wine will travel to Kentucky, Samoa and Shantung, to Trollhättan in Sweden and to the Ivory Coast. The *pesos* they collect from that are what will really add zest to the pot of cabbage.

"Nonetheless, our figures are not coming up right," said Hein Schäffers. "In the fall two hundred settler families will be arriving from Poland and Bukovina. Potatoes will be keeping us company for five more years at least. In San Juan last fall they let two hundred thousand liters of the very best red wine run off into the irrigation ditches because people have to pay more for water than what the agents are willing to lay out for even the best red wine. We'll have to stick with potatoes for a while, I think, and feed ourselves with honest work. We do have a jump on the new people, though, and it's not one they can make up for in five years.

"Furthermore not long ago we all sat down and decided to put in a school, for the children naturally. You could become a teacher if your papers are in order. We do have to verify that everything for the children is properly documented. We still haven't received the authorization from the school inspector though."

"Hein, my friend, if that fails to come through, then your children won't be learning to read and write until they're in the army. In this part of the world *mañana* means ten years from now. In my case whether or not I stay a while longer among the quail and draw the furrows for the grape shoots depends ultimately on the friendly larks in my head. Or else on whether I see if my papers are in the order that you demand for those runny-nosed little kids of yours."

In fact Johann Peter Langfoot had meant to stay for only four weeks. However it had now been four months since he had been hanging around. In the meantime he had inherited a pair of black wool trousers with white stripes and a flannel shirt like those the *gauchos* wear, set off by either a bright red or a sky blue neckerchief. Thus freshly decked out, he set off for the village.

The man at the store had to chalk up a full three *cañas* for Langfoot. And with that Johann Peter walked out; and there wasn't even a wobble in his gait. He didn't go to Hein Schäffers ranch right away either. The moon shone on the fields as bright as day. The cormorants and herons could be heard screeching by the lagoon. Either there's a puma prowling around or some wretched old yacaré has bitten a flamingo in the leg. The swarm of birds swirled noisily over the silvery surface of the water like a black rain cloud. There was scarcely space for the moon. In a clearing among the reeds Johann Peter Langfoot had baited two hooks for turtles. The meat was gone and so were the turtles. The water fowl continued to swirl drunkenly through the air. Looking out from a rock, Johann Peter Langfoot could see straight across the water, and finally he discovered the monstrous yacaré. It had not yet made its move, but it was eager to do so. The herons and flamingos were just not doing him the favor of putting their legs within reach of his jaws.

Johann Peter Langfoot had lost interest. The birds in his head were chirping up a storm.... If I could at least count on a woman for tonight. But it's another two hundred kilometers to where I'd have my pick of all the pleasures in San Juan. And many a night will yet be spent getting there.

He caught himself a big firefly, took its head between his fingers, and let the tail section illuminate his way. As he went along, he sang this song which someone had apparently thought up while weeding:

In this land of air untainted
It's said starvation takes no toll;
Our former digs we therefore traded
And found ourselves a brand new hole.

What every one must know
Is like a worm to slither;
With stomach fully stretched
To dine on grass for dinner.

It wasn't just for fun, you see
That God turned brambles sharp and hard
And once a man has fed on these
They'll be his home once he's expired.

From out the corpse will grow
Fresh weeds and cheerful holly;
The sun rose gray at dawn,
 And now it sinks, still cloudy.

There's nothing left that's colored red,
And nary a local had reddish skin;

But seeing red, men shot these dead,
To make gold pickings an easier win.

The "red" have since turned gray.
Their lives today in shambles,
One often finds the *indios*
With wind to eat, not brambles.

But Hein Schäffers had another one of those hangovers as he sat crouched in front of his *rancho* with his hands folded thinking of the linden trees on the Rhine. He too was singing a song and his eyes had turned misty.

"Yes indeed, old friend … ," said Johann Peter Langfoot, "I have also been wishing for something soft to spend the night with. But even if we could bring it in here by air, it would be stale by the time it arrived." He went into the shack, quietly packed his junk, and said to Hein Schäffers, "Well if you ever need another dummy to hack the weeds out of your potatoes, catch your quail and keep the locusts from attacking your person, … you know where to find me. Good luck!"

Hein Schäffers walked along with him for quite a distance and promised him twenty percent of whatever the harvest brought in. Let him not rush off like a fool. And what about the good chance he had of becoming their teacher? Indian women were as plentiful as quail. Plus, without the locusts, even this was going to be a record year for tobacco and *caña*.

In the meantime they had arrived at the *almacén* where Jochen Peltzer and Timm Timmermann were soaking their dandy hangover in *caña* and thrashing around with playing cards at the table.

"Let's at least drink another in honor of your departure," urged Hein Schäffers. But that was not in any way Langfoot's intention. And if it wasn't his intention…. But he said: "Hey, Hein, I owe that rascal of a shopkeeper for three *cañas*. Each of you three now drink another two to my health. Pay the check from the percentages. And for all I care, you can shove the rest!"

He was also much quicker on his feet than Hein Schäffers, who tried to hold him back by the collar. A truck came rolling down the highway. In a flash Langfoot was on top. There was no straighter way to San Juan. And as he crouched up there on the potato sacks, he thought to himself, "So you send potatoes to San Juan. The stringless wax beans. The peanuts. The blue wine and the red. And when Langfoot sets off in that direction, or I should say when the potato truck simply carries him off, should the sun suddenly come to a standstill in Terrabussa Valley?"

The moon shone down on his contentedly sleeping face. And on its way earthward a shooting star nearly grazed the locks on his head which the wind had already disheveled.

Chapter Twelve

The steam being produced up and down the entire Paraná River by the heat was like that in a Russian sauna. Everyone who was a passenger lay on the upper deck beneath the suspended cloth and gasped for a breath of cool air. But where was it to come from? The river had cut its bed deep between two steep walls of dense jungle. Alligators with a mighty wish to moisten their rugged skin slipped back into the water with a swishing sound. It was the kind of water that looked boggy and produced streams of foul smelling gases as if some sort of wartime marmalade made of turnip cabbage and oxblood had begun to ferment. The trail of foam made by the paddle wheels remained on the water for an eternity and split the wide surface of the water in two. On close observation you could almost believe that the left side was aglow in a blaze of red orchids and the right side had draped itself in a light veil of bluish gray gauze. This had probably been caused by the clouds, which were flying very high and weren't indicative of rain. However, it could also be attributed to the multicolored treetops that displayed every imaginable hue in their leafy boughs. But Langfoot was too lazy to rack his brain on that subject for long. And the only thought that still occupied a choice seat in his noisy noggin had coiled itself around his craving for ice cold drinks, excluding most anything else. But this glorified coffee grinder of a ship had not yet progressed to the point of serving the more refined segment of civilization. The cattle breeders and assorted other *estancieros* did not make demands until Paris or the Riviera. Still finer tastes did not develop in them until they moved up to ambassadorships in London or Madrid, appointments which, needless to say, each of these *caballeros* carried with him in the hip pocket of his *bombachas*. At the ship's bar the most you could expect to find was ice-chilled brandy that was lukewarm anyway, tasted like paprika and parsley, and caused big boils to form on the tongue. The craftiest passengers were sucking on *mate* straws. One exceptionally bright fellow had mixed the *yerba* with peppermint.

A cute little jungle flower, decked out city style, with sparkling slanted eyes and fluttering, raven black hair was toying with an orange the size of a child's head. She didn't have the strength left, nor perhaps the will, to peel it although her fingernails certainly had the correct proportions for the task. She simply bit into it as if it were an apple and, after sucking out the pulp, spit the pieces out against the wall of the pilot house. The searing heat nailed the offal firmly to the wall. An entire row of similarly expectorated orange pulp nailings already studded the sheet metal housing. But otherwise the young lady had quite a charming mouth – especially in the event it ever came to making affectionate moves – including big, straight teeth and an inordinately strong chin to match. In her bright red sunsuit she shone like a burning bramble bush. Here, in the land of four men to each of the women. Women who submit to all four but who don't belong to a single one. In this land, however, the mysterious doña had little to gain from doing her act with the red scarf. Whatever there was aboard that ship that looked like a man merely let his eyes sink steadily lower in introspection or else turned them loose in the jungle to rustle up the wind, let's say, or some iceberg that had been buried long ago by the Incas.

From within the jungle there occasionally emerged scarlet and azure tanagers. The herons looked as if the ovenlike heat had scorched their feathers. Pelicans protruded wearily from the grassy islets. They were probably not real pelicans, but they managed to look like pelicans anyway when the wake soaked them with dirty foam. Out of the reeds shot forth redtailed thrushes and yellow-green sea gulls with black heads. The racket they were making gave way to a hellish cacophony of primeval proportions. They seemed angry at being disturbed. And yet a clumsy motorized vehicle like ours would only pass near their nesting places once every four days.

The *señorita* in the red nylon dress really should be a little ashamed, with her elegant pale makeup and unwashed neck, grumbled Langfoot. She's parading around strung with all the trappings of a black mammy from Ubacahua. But we're in a civilized region here, and our not exactly backward taste prefers small round Manzanillo cigars. Furthermore, cotton slippers with yellow pompoms are not the appropriate thing to wear deckside with a sunsuit; elegant pumps made of scarlet red Moroccan leather would be more like it. There's even an onion as thick as my fist stuck to her left foot. Too bad, my darling! Himself, on the other hand, Johann Peter Langfoot perceived as being quite nattily attired, with his yellow raw silk shirt and his brown flannel trousers, his smoothly shaven

Mr. Churchill face and his gray temples. He just couldn't muster much respect for the heat. Nonetheless he had thought in time of chewing gum, and consequently he was managing quite well thus far. If only the *señorita* were not equipped with quite so much flab from her shoulders down to her calves ... , then maybe he would have allowed himself the honor of helping her kill some of the time of which she appeared to have so much on her hands and with which she seemed not to know what to do. Now she was spitting peanut shells through the air in a high curve until they hit the water, taking no notice whatsoever of the fish that were snapping at them below.

Johann Peter Langfoot was on his way down from Asunción and had a pocket full of gold. He had fallen in with some smugglers and had made a corresponding bundle in no time at all. In the future, however, he was not planning to continue scavenging around like a sneaky dog. Three minutes before the customs officials raided the shack and nabbed the entire band of criminals he had stepped out the door; he had sensed that something unusual was in the wind and had immediately grabbed the horse by the reins. The animal belonged to the authorities, it's true, but one has to be blessed with a certain amount of luck to move ahead rapidly. And at present he was hunting some other type of luck. He also believed that he now had a clear notion of which paths were best for this hunt. The disgusting heat, however, made his brain as brackish as it did the waters of the Paraná below. These looked like what is known as 'clear' turtle soup. Given the choice, a person would rather bite into a lemon. Not a single lemon could be found aboard ship, not even one bitter orange.

Aside from the *señorita*, whose chapter Johann Peter Langfoot therewith closed without having included himself in it, the other person lying around was a practically bald and otherwise extremely rundown *caballero* in a faded pair of purple pajamas. He will probably be forced to think of this dismal journey for quite a while. Why? Because he wasn't able to cover his costs. This was a gambler by trade, and a crooked one at that. Under the right conditions he had the ability to hoodwink unsuspecting gamblers with such dexterity that not even he would sometimes notice when something slipped out of his cuff. The phony ten of spades, for instance, the marked ace, the notched queen of hearts, and the double ten of diamonds. But in this hellish hotpot no one was exactly driven to lose his lunch money in such an utterly painless fashion. They might possibly have bowled or thrown the ball around a couple of times ... , but cards took too much effort.

The *caballero* in the purple pajamas was suffering from acute boredom. There was no more room at the jawbone for him to yawn. He could not even drum up enough of an appetite to take a bite out of the conveniently placed *señorita*, who was actively making passes at him with her gleaming, round, penetrating brown eyes because she secretly suspected that he was a cattle baron or, at the very least, the owner of a rice plantation. In the meantime she had pegged Langfoot for a shameless Scotsman or for an oil prospector out of Boston. The *caballero* was smoking small blond tobacco cigarettes made in Manila while simultaneously conversing in Portuguese with a young man of identically leathern complexion on the subjects of butterflies, orchids, and ritual African dances. He made casual mention of his intention to undertake a special side trip to Rio in a few weeks. The way he put it, he had only seen the widely touted Sugarloaf by the gray of morning, and it had at the time made the impression of a drowsy nightcap jammed over a reluctant sea monster. A long time ago on that beautiful rainy day in May the 'Monte Olivia' was sailing past it with four hundred third class passengers. His paramour for the four nights that separated Pernambuco from Rio was a woman named Alma Maria, who was headed back into the arms of her rightful husband as soon as she arrived in Rio Grande, where she would be met on the spot by dew-laden roses, the squeals of Negresses, and three cute, little, flaxen-haired boys still unmistakably Austrian in their speech and in their tears.

In those days Johann Peter's birds were not yet cavorting as obstreperously inside his brain. Back then he still had German currency in his chest pouch. That was when Montevideo was still a city where you could convert your bills into Uruguayan *pesos* for pretty decent money. The Peludo Bar was still on the *plaza* then with its regular lineup of beastly women in every possible shade of skin. This was where the unsuspecting were sold bubbly apple wine for authentic French champagne. The barkeep, don Isidoro, possessed the smartest mouth this continent was ever blessed to have. "May as well write off that little dalliance!" said Johann Peter; for even today that account remained unsettled. The last man who had rolled his eyes and expressed dismay had ended up among those who headed home. His final words before safely retiring to a plush stateroom on the 'Cape Arcona' were: "Johann Peter, ... buddy, why are you constantly asking yourself whether your soul is among the redeemed or whether it is rotten to the core? Why do you take it all so seriously anyway? If this is how you feel, then you should calmly live out your life in this monkey paradise. But for heaven's sake, don't blame it on me. I'm lifting anchor as you see. Don't let anything happen to those birds! I'll see you sometime when they've tired of thrashing about and no longer expose parts of their body to further injury...."

This farewell sermon had completely failed to serve its purpose. Nothing of either sort was important to Johann Peter anymore, not salvation nor damnation. He was not like some tree obliged to live without freedom. What true freedom means was something the birds were teaching him. And for the time being, at least, he was unable to do without them.

In the water below everything swam in a bloody stream that gushed from a bed of algae. The sun was of a good mind to drown there. She was wearing a dress of lavender gray clouds. Her tired face gave off a matte reflection as if through a window smeared with lipstick. There was an unusual smell of camphor in the air and the boulders on the shore were soft and vulnerable like the flesh of a virgin.

Langfoot lay as if suffering from alcohol poisoning for three days following this nautical adventure. He was stretched out in a bright, sunny room with pastel drapes and beige wallpaper. He would alternately chew on ice and gag on aspirin tablets. He drank peppermint tea by the liter and ladled down some sort of calf's broth. Stacks of newspapers were piled on the thin linen blanket of his bed yet because of the sheer number of letters he could not make rhyme or reason of what was being served up for the consumption of the loyal municipal and provincial subscribers. The landlady found Langfoot's state of health concerning. The doctor prescribed quinine. Johann Peter would spit the white powder out into the chamber pot and eat seven bockwursts along with a potful of sauerkraut. Eventually that caused Langfoot's brain to resume a moderately reasonable course. The newspapers were audibly crackling with reports of much worse times to come. To remain above all that you had to be either twenty years of age or past eighty. Johann Peter just happened to have taken up residence in the wrong generation. It was the most tragic one in centuries. He concluded: "Well, so what! The main thing is not to put on weight and to redeem your last vouchers!"

Johann Peter Langfoot figured up his present net worth. It consisted of a chest pouch grown greasy with wear and its seven hundred and nine Argentinean *peso* contents, valued at one hundred and eighty-nine U.S. dollars. He walked up *Colón* Avenue and back down *Defensa*. The time had come to look around for a profitable business.

He liked the city even less than he had two years earlier. The many idle people sitting around on benches got on his nerves. It bugged him to see all those people incessantly buying the latest edition of the newspaper. And all those people going for a spin in fabulously beautiful automobiles with silver trim and antennae, flower vases and warm water faucets, and a correspondingly attired Rosita or Haydée at their side, thinking at each intersection about their long overdue installments; all of it made the birds in his throbbing brain grow rebellious again.

As he passed by a shoeshine stand, he remembered the juniper bush he had lain under in Germany once in September when the heath was red and the four weeks of school vacation were coming to an end. His grandfather August owned twenty head of sheep and thirty-three beehives. From the sheep and the hives were derived the silver coins that tuition and especially the drinking sprees in Heidelberg devoured. Grandfather August could see the inevitable. He could tell that one day, like some professional drifter who makes a wide circle around every job, his sorriest grandchild would be done in out on the highway by the birds that he had allowed to be planted in his head.

Just before Langfoot was almost sent through a plate glass window by a reckless fruit vendor and his two heavy baskets of oranges and bananas, he was thinking of that final hour in Berlin when the dancer Olivera swept past him, slender as a gazelle, gave him a big, wide-eyed look, and still did not greet him. Why? Well, why should anyone weep, as the song goes, "when the other one is already standing on the next corner ... ?"

Johann Peter Langfoot could have gone on forever thinking about experiences, far and near, of this type ... right on past the month of December, through January, and into February. The humidity in the air stood at ninety-nine percent. A cigar required the use of half a box of matches before it reached the point of being discarded. On the *Calle Florida* meanwhile a certain individual continued to wear down his corns. At present he had just eleven *pesos*, forty *centavos* in his pocket and owed half a month on his rent. And on top of that next Saturday the 'Boca Juniors' were facing off against the 'River Plate' team for the league championship. (Soccer under police supervision; referees are worked over; goalie position is occupied by a Brazilian Negro who cost the team thirty-five thousand *pesos* cash – and who for that sinfully extravagant amount of money couldn't even fly higher than the corner kicks that slipped into his goal.)

Still, on the way to the subway it occurred to Johann Peter Langfoot that according to an advertisement in *La Crítica* they were looking for a young man to fit and tint inkpads. He decided he would not apply for this particular vacancy. Instead he went to have a cup of black coffee.

Chapter Thirteen

Once long ago Johann Peter had struck pay dirt while having the black brew, for that had led to a conversation with the head accountant at the Ellermann Company. The conversation had lasted two hours and ended in dinner together and Langfoot receiving a thirty *peso* 'advance' on a position in the offices of the Ellermann Export firm. Four days later Johann Peter assumed his duties as French and German correspondent, netting him a monthly income of one hundred and eighty *pesos*. We won't burden the reader unnecessarily by detailing the somersaults performed by every bird assembled in the head of this human host of theirs. In fact their combined highjinks lasted quite a long time and only ended when Rosita ceased to be around. Actually she was still physically present, but her body was no longer exclusively there for Johann Peter. We all know, however, that he had never any intention of emulating Othello. Locally he was known as Juan; he forbade everyone the use of the 'don' title. He wouldn't even allow the women to use it though they didn't exactly go out of their way to avoid him, and he was by no means one to make detours either.

But two years' time had already passed under that bridge. Rosita seemed to feel quite at home in the house of her well-paying *caballeros*. Ellermann and Company had gone the way of all flesh. And so Johann Peter found himself once again seated before a cup of black coffee imagining that by rights this should be a lucky day. Johann Peter Langfoot treated himself to the intended cup of coffee and then to a glass of beer in a *boliche* on the *Calle Balcarce*. The owner of this dive, which was frequented primarily by Germans, was Julio Murr.

Since the fan was on the blink again, special guests were seated outside around six metal tables that stood beneath the mighty limbs of a single *ombú* tree.

The huge, leafy mass of the treetop created an umbrella of proportions that are unimaginable to a European. This particular evening brought with it such a wave of heat that without the shade of a tree only a person with an ice pack on his skull could more or less make it.

Julio Murr had taken a break and left the drudgery to the bartender and to Jesús, the one-eyed waiter. He had taken a seat at the table of his friend Johann Peter and had shifted his talkativeness into high gear. His opponent was in equally top form. The birds were sound asleep. The four *pesos* made daily by packing and delivering were all the more flighty. What was left over only managed to fill the chest pouch *poco a poco*.

Just as Johann Peter was planning to put the glass to his mouth to toast Julio Murr, a shoeblack poked his head around the corner, haltingly made his way up to the gnarled base of the tree, and pretended to be verifying something that had previously given him a mild fright. Then he closed one eye, shook himself, and disappeared again.

Johann Peter spit to one side, at least partially hitting the toe of his boot with the spittle, and his nose turned blue: "Damn that lowlife!"

Julio looked up and asked, "Are you seeing white mice already, Peter?"

"Yes," growled Johann Peter, "that was of course him. Without any doubt. I needed only to close my left eye, ... he knew immediately and closed his right eye."

"Is he someone I know? He did look like one of our people, obviously."

"Maybe you do know him. This may also be the last time he ever shows his face around here. Because he's a coward on top of everything else, you know."

"Then he must have already been up to quite a lot of mischief if he can get you this upset. But I'm of the opinion that a person shouldn't keep holding a grudge against someone who did him a bad turn, especially if it's one of our own people. Just give the slate a few brisk strokes with an eraser, and let the poor devil keep his slice of the pie. The bootblacking, I mean."

"If it were only that ... , he could shine on to his heart's content for all I care. Even though a sour taste comes to my tongue when I see one of our people with a shoeshine kit. Yet I have to admit that there haven't been many – even counting my insignificant self – who have crossed my path as bootblacks."

"My God, I'll admit it's not pleasant to see one of our own on a corner like that, Peter. But when you really sit down and think about it, then it's all just the same. Whether you're polishing boots or washing dishes, whether it's corn, wheat, or cattle you're speculating in, or whatever the kind of land you may be pushing, work is work, even for our people. Furthermore, if you have no job and don't want to turn Catholic ... , our high and mighty gentry isn't the least bit willing to let you bleed them easily for a *peso*. They only make donations when it gets into the newspapers."

"Naturally. Work is work. That's one thing you sure don't have to tell me. You take the jobs whenever they turn up. But when a guy is trafficking in women … , that's going too far. And he was selling them all right. Zumbusch was trafficking in women."

"Zumbusch it was, you say?" asked Julio Murr.

"Yes … , Hein Zumbusch. When we were still with Ellermann he and I would come here every afternoon for our cup of black coffee."

"Now it's coming back to me. I remember exactly how furious you became when Ellermann and Co. went bankrupt overnight. But you had another job within two weeks, didn't you?"

"Quite the opposite. I loafed around for two months without work. My savings were eaten up, and all the while I'm pulling this guy Zumbusch through with me. And that's when the big con job took place."

"With Zumbusch?"

"With Zumbusch, Rosita … , you name it."

"Rosita? You've never told me anything about that, Peter."

"Well, back then things had not yet reached a stage where you could do much talking about them. I mean, Rosita and I had pretty much reached an understanding. And if the Ellermanns hadn't been forced to close their store, our formal engagement, with all the appropriate hoopla, was bound to take place."

"Now either do me the favor of telling the entire story, or keep the whole kit and caboodle to yourself. Who is Rosita, why did your engagement to her not take place, and what has Zumbusch got to do with it?"

"Yes, I guess I do owe you that much. So here goes the story: Rosita was a sales clerk in a men's store on Corrientes Street. She wasn't a local. God forbid! You know that I've never been partial to the type that smells of carnations and carries the jungle under her armpits. Rosita was the perfect picture of a girl. Snow white skin and amber eyes. Red hair. Completely my type. I'd have done any number of foolish things for her. Actually I only came into the store by pure chance.… Wanted to buy myself a tie, that's all. Rosita brought some out. She spoke German right off. We got into a conversation. From business it went to private. And then suddenly every Saturday I needed ties, shirt collars, or socks. Afterwards I could have opened my own store with it all. And from a conversation in the store to a friendly chat at the café was certainly no tremendous leap. You know, things took their natural course.… Then we strolled around the Palermo district and went on an outing to Tigre. We attended balls and took part in shipboard parties. We also attended the *Colón* Theater together a couple of times. That kind of entertainment doesn't come cheap: Italian opera, German opera. There went ten *pesos* every time. Her mother, to whom the store belonged, had no objections even though I was one of the goyim and Rosita was from Eastern Poland. This was real love at first sight, despite everything. I didn't even mention the bleak outlook at Ellermann's since I reasoned that I was sure to have another job within a week or so. I told myself that I'd probably even be earning fifty *pesos* more a month. And once or twice I took Zumbusch shopping with me too. I wanted him to get the same discount as I did of course. For a tie that normally cost five *pesos* he only had to pay three if Rosita was there. Once or twice she also exchanged a few words with him, the way people do. And occasionally he would try to make her laugh. But that was all that ever happened.

"We were, on the whole, hanging around together a lot at this time. He would run out of money right away. At first all I did was spring for his beer or his coffee. Pretty soon it was his meal too. Heck, by the end it was me who bailed him out with the landlady; we were living in the same boarding house, you see. Otherwise he'd have skipped out. But after six weeks of watching the mooching act wear on, I told myself that it was time to make a quick end of this would-be retirement of his! Now, my friend, whatever job comes along is the one you take. It's essential that we make it through the winter. Unfortunately Zumbusch had no notion whatsoever of how to latch on to a paying job in a hurry. He just kept waiting for 'the big one.' And the dirty dog didn't even buy lottery tickets either. This was something he had already learned from the natives, who dream of the jackpot night after night without having made a contribution. But they do paint themselves this mental picture of how it will be when they're holding about half a million *pesos* in their pocket and begin making the rounds of all the whorehouses. And how they then ask the liveliest girl out for a movie on Lavalle Street.

"But Zumbusch.... Well, let's not talk about what he dreamed up. Where was he supposed to get the price of a lottery ticket? I never gave him any cash money. Even though he'd frequently try to hit me up for some. He has never had any scruples with respect to that.

"So, ... that's when I came up with the idea to give the fields a try. This was neither a great, nor a new idea. But we had no options. And I said to Zumbusch: 'Hey, the smartest thing for us to do is for us both to hit the corn. We'll get something to eat out there. And under the right conditions, we can make a bundle of money.'

"'Why not?' Zumbusch said. 'But I don't have the right clothes for the fields. All I have is this suit here. And it'll be done for in a matter of weeks. Beyond that, the only other things I have are these shoes and this shirt.'

"'Good,' I replied. 'What you need for the fields we'll be able to come up with down the way at the cheap Jewish place.' What I was thinking to myself was: This fellow is still one of our people, after all. The good Lord is not going to help, and the *Deutscher Klub* is still less likely to, even though he once wrote them a letter begging for money. I kept thinking to myself: Who knows if you might not some day find yourself in a similar predicament again. One should help if one can. Fine, … I helped. I don't have any illusions about it. It's just a fact. We worked it out so that he was to pay back the cash I had advanced him with the money earned picking crops. And not until the end either. At the employment office things clicked right away. We were to be ready to travel in three days. Expenses and the price of our tickets were advanced to us by the employment broker on behalf of the boss. In those days that was customary here.

"I gave Rosita a long story about how I had to make a trip through the Northern provinces in connection with work. It could last two months, perhaps even three, depending on the circumstances. Together, we enjoyed one last grand farewell dinner at the establishment owned by chubby Hannes Käsebieter. I bought her a charming silver stickpin, an antique Peruvian piece. But after I had already bought the thing, it dawned on me that one should never give a gift that is sharp or pointed; it'll punch holes in your love life. But I said to myself: What better time than this! In fact, she didn't make the farewell as agonizingly difficult for me as what I had imagined deep down. That really should have caught my attention. Maybe the trip was already too much on my mind. And then too, you always think you've got things sewed up when a girl who didn't jump right into bed with you has finally been won over. That night we didn't part much differently than when we had said 'good night' to one another in the past. A kiss. And another kiss. And to conclude, one more that I placed on her red hair taking a nibble as I went. Maybe she also had tears in her eyes. I don't know any more. In any case I was completely choked up.

"Zumbusch whistled a tune as we departed, and late on the second day we landed at the *chacra*. The farm belonged to a Spaniard named Ceballos Carcama. A nice old man. His wife was a nice old lady too. Their son was half retarded but harmless. He passed himself off as the chief *gaucho* with silver spurs the size of plates and a sky blue poncho. In his belt were an ancient sword and two guns inlaid with gold and mother of pearl. They served us a very decent meal. Initially it was impossible to demolish the servings of meat we were given. But you become accustomed to them before long and are then eating about a fourth of a steer every day. For us to sleep they had fixed up some bedding in the ranch hands' *galpón*. I was oblivious to the vermin. And since there was no electricity and we could therefore not have any light, the mosquitos left us alone. But the first thing Zumbusch said as we were stretching out on the corn straw was: 'You know, Peter, I feel like a prisoner now. The only thing still missing is a ball and chain on each leg.'

"That rankled me all to hell. And I didn't respond for that very reason.

"The first day in the cornfields was certainly no piece of cake. I worked my hands to the bone. But I always stayed close behind the two Indian women so as to latch on to the tricks of the trade right away. Naturally I also wound up with half the normal quota. I gave this some thought: The pay is only likely to be this meager today and maybe tomorrow as well. Day after tomorrow I'll start competing equally with the others. We'll see then whether a white man can't also, in addition to having quicker wits than these native people, be swifter with his hands. In my zeal for work I completely stopped worrying about Zumbusch at first. He was the last man on the picking line. He was infinitely behind. And that evening he said to me: 'Hey, Peter, if things don't go any smoother tomorrow, then you can fish me out of the lagoon. No joke, I'm really jumping in. This is absolutely unbearable.' I had a good long talk with him, much like when the local *indios* whisper a long proverb into a mule's ear if it suddenly starts to balk and won't budge at any price. But after the little talk the mule walks. And afterwards the boss also invited us all to share a drink of Pisco with him; it almost burned away half your throat. A night's rest took care of everything else.

"The second night Zumbusch gave an even crazier performance. 'We're even worse off than prisoners,' he complained. 'At least they know why they must shoulder their crosses. But would you please explain to me what it is I'm guilty of that would require such penance of me here?'

"This time it was the *gaucho* who stopped his yapping. He strummed something on the guitar for him and ran through a couple of scratchy camp songs with his tinny voice … to the point that the bats came to a flying standstill like frozen fragments of night. And then a sharp wind came up and drove dust into our faces until our eyelids stuck to our eyeballs. And sleep didn't keep us waiting for long. The only thing I could still think was: Today you were almost keeping up with the women's pace. Langpfötchen, my boy, this thing is starting to shape up.

"At about noon on the third day, just after I had flung myself onto a haystack to take a little nap, Zumbusch came running up screaming as if he had a scorpion's stinger stuck in his butt.

"'You know,' he said, 'someone really ought to put a bullet through you right now, like a mad dog. What a fine kettle of fish you've cooked up for me here! How's this for you: I'm supposed to break my back here over a period of twelve hours and get fifty *centavos*? Tearing up my clothes.

Ripping the flesh from my bones! Am I guilty of murder? Am I some kind of scoundrel?'

"'Hey, it worked out to a *peso* twenty for me yesterday. Today I'm sure to make it up to two *pesos*. And next week there won't be a day under four.'

"'With kernels that are this small, what you're going to get is crap. And most of the cobs are just half full. Is this stuff corn at all? It could be mistaken for poppy seeds.'

"'When we get to the next section, down closer to the lagoon, the cobs will be twice this size. And you can still be sure of earning your three *pesos*. Aside from that, you need to put a little more effort into your picking. Not be standing around all the time watching the clouds instead.'

"'The Italian said field hands in Córdoba get an average of five *pesos*.'

"'Then I'm surprised he's still hanging around here.'

"'The truth is he wants to skip out next Monday. And I'll be going with him.'

"'I can't stop you from going. But then it's not nice of you to put me in a bad light around here either.'

"'You're welcome to come too. I never said you should stay behind alone.'

"'We just can't pull out on the boss in the middle of his harvest. Furthermore it's a sneaky breach of contract for us to leave before the time has elapsed that was agreed upon.'

"'Breach of contract?'

"'Yes. We've committed ourselves to at least fourteen days. And the harvest doesn't last much longer than that anyway. We'll be moving on to other pastures then as it is. And by that time you'll also have mastered the picking process.'

"'What a numskull I was to have listened to you! There can't be any decent people signing up for field work. Decent people are able to make a living in the city.'

"'I've had ample opportunity to observe your inability to make an honest living in the city. And to my mind no job is indecent if it feeds me. However if I have a job and throw it away for no plausible reason, I'm the indecent one.'

"'These people are the worst kind of exploiters though; that cancels out any good faith or loyalty.'

"'The city has plenty of that sort too, chum.'

"'But after all in town I was making a hundred and twenty *pesos* a month. Here I'll be lucky if I get thirty.'

"'Fine. But what would you have earned in the city today?'"

"'But don't you understand? I don't want to be here anymore! I'd rather scrape my meals together in town out of a trash can or something. Am I some Chinese coolie? Did my mother just drop me in some ditch?'

"'Hey, I didn't come into the world on a dung heap either! And even if that were the case, what difference could it possibly make in any of this?'

"'Have you no pride? You're forgetting that you are a German.'

"'I don't get that. How do you mean?'

"'That we should be accepting the lowliest jobs from these crappy farmers who can't even read or write. And that we're expected to say thank you on top of it. And if you continue to be headstrong like some billy goat, knowing full well what I mean, then I'll go ahead and take off tonight, that's all.'

"'Well, all right. Let's wait until later this evening. Once we've settled down, we'll think about what needs to be done. Nonetheless, I know for my part that there's really no sound reason for us to pick up stakes again and commit breach of contract in the process.'

"'As far as it concerns these idiots, no contract is binding. But all right; I'll let this ride until tonight. You certainly won't be seeing any more of me come morning though.'

"He walked away frowning. A big red butterfly was fluttering along ahead of him. He chased after it. I went back into the corn patch and didn't see him again until we were preparing to demolish our supper. I do believe he loafed around all afternoon and didn't even make thirty *centavos*.

"After dinner he chewed my ear off for two solid hours. Time after time he would emphasize how we had gotten into it over our ears here. And if I was dumb enough to want to keep working for less than nothing, I'd simply be seen as a strike breaker. Yes, it was his damned duty and obligation to enlighten me. Everyone needed to be enlightened here. By the same token he thought it was a shame there was no type of union here. In Córdoba we were sure to end up in friendlier hands. He knew the address of an employment broker too; the Italian had given it to him. And the Italian would be catching up in a couple of days. I found it impossible to talk him out of his foolish plan. Besides, I was too tired to keep on arguing with him about it. Once when I was most vulnerable, I finally said, 'yes.' He took me immediately at my word. Now I couldn't go back on it. We therefore decided to make our run for it just as dusk set in. That way we'd reach the next rail station before anyone discovered we had escaped. In accordance with conventional camp laws the boss had the right to use force to make us abide by the contract. He could have us chased down by the *gauchos* and captured like cattle intended for the slaughterhouse. They'd be cracking the bullwhip at our ears every step of the way back. And there would be no justice anywhere for us – only for the boss. While I was making him aware of these assorted eventualities, Zumbusch showed no sign of being at all impressed.

"Fine. We lay awake in our bunks until it began to get dark. We had no luggage; the few belongings we had could be stashed in our pockets. We made it off the farm unnoticed. A slight mist still lay over the fields. Dew was dripping from the corn stalks and wetting us through and through as if the clouds had burst on us. Zumbusch was constantly gasping for air; he felt his heart beating in his throat. For my part, my gut felt like it had an enormous half ton boulder sitting in there. Behind the lagoon the sun was coming up. The moon could also still be seen. We now had tall grass in front of us for a change. The hard spikelets slashed at our faces. Water gushed through our shoes while up top we were being scorched. I could see Zumbusch holding back tears. He was stumbling even more than walking. A couple of excited *ñandús* made a beeline for us. Zumbusch turned sharply to the left and promptly toppled over. It was a good thing too; the legs of the winged runners more than just nicked him. I was slapped by a faceful of dust and feathers. The sun had finally pierced the thick formation of clouds. But there was no sign of a train depot. To have struck out in the wrong direction meant the *gauchos* were bound to catch up with us. Once again we had to circle around a lagoon. In their haste to take flight the herons created a riotous commotion. I'd have gladly taken a sip of water, but the entire lagoon was boggy. Dozens of yacarés lay there, their crocodilian mouths gaping. A fiery red flamingo stood atop a giant turtle. I would have enjoyed seeing it at closer range, but it was impossible to get even one step nearer. On the other side of the lagoon the acreage of another *chacra* began. Here the corn was actually twice the size. The rows were marching into the sun like a regiment of soldiers. Light was reflecting off the swordlike leaves with a yellowish-white, phosphorescent shimmer. Billions of cicadas were out there chirping on them. Around the tops of the nearly six-foot stalks the evaporating dew hovered like a cloud. We were enveloped by an ovenlike sultriness. I could no longer close my mouth. A man's tongue felt dry as tree bark lying up against the dehydrated roof of his mouth. We had perhaps been on the move for four hours when we finally saw the Quonset hut that passed for a railroad station. I turned around at the embankment and looked back in the direction that we had come to see if they were already on our trail. But far and wide no riders were discernible. If we just made it onto the railhead and got hold of our tickets, then the *gauchos* would have nothing on us; then we'd be guests of the rail company. Only a few more bounding leaps – and we were up. I had just enough money to make it to Córdoba. We bought our tickets and within ten minutes the train pulled in. I nearly had to carry Zumbusch aboard. It was as if all his muscles were paralyzed. Luckily the compartment was completely empty. We could stretch wherever and however we wished. According to the conductor we'd be in Córdoba in four hours. Four hours of sleep. That will refresh us, I thought to myself. It will also dry us out from head to toe too. At the time, you see, we looked like walking scarecrows, all filthy and torn. If someone were to have caught sight of us in that condition on the road, he'd have made a big circle around us. Oh well, what could be the point in dwelling on that.... Zumbusch was already snoring on the other side of the seat; he probably hadn't given a moment's thought to anything. Finally I closed my eyes too and slept as if I were in a feather bed three feet thick.

"When I woke up I was surrounded by the black impenetrability of night, and my teeth were chattering for cold. I needed a good ten minutes to straighten out my thoughts. And when I was finally able to sit up and touch my surroundings, I noticed that I was still lying on the seat. The train was standing still. I could hear the whistling of locomotives. At last I managed to get on my feet. I searched for a window, let it down, and discovered that I was surrounded by a maze of rails and endless rows of freight cars. So this had to be a rail yard. And far off in the distance I also saw the lights of a railroad station. At this point Zumbusch popped into my mind. I called and called. I called three, four times. No answer. I felt around on the seats, on the floor; I went out on the platform. There wasn't a trace of Zumbusch to be found. Then I thought for a good while and gradually came to the realization that I must have slept not four hours, but fourteen. I wanted to light a match to look at the time; dripping wet. I couldn't feel the position of the hands. I looked all over the rail car again. Zumbusch had transformed himself into a spirit, and the spirit had vanished into nothing. I was none the wiser after looking the rail car over from outside. In any case I now knew that it had been uncoupled. But where? Where had the sequence of world events taken me? And how could it be that I should be stumbling around here alone among the rails and that Zumbusch was not with me?

"After half an hour I had at least found out that this was the rail depot of Santa Fe. And after another half hour I was huddled in a *boliche*, slinging a massive *puchero* down my throat. It was already approaching midnight, and it was pointless to look for Zumbusch around here. The boss, a man from Portugal, let me bunk down in the stable. I got no sleep, however; the spook of Zumbusch was knocking around in my head. Had that rat allowed me to sleep quietly on in Córdoba and then silently, surreptitiously crept away? That would truly be an underhanded trick. And as it turned out, it was. In any case I was now sitting fast in Santa Fe, Argentina.

"I didn't need to look around for an employment broker very long at all. One of them had opened his office right next to the *boliche*. He said I came to him like the answer to a prayer. There was, on a *chacra* ten kilometers from there, more work than there were people to do it. He prepared the contract, and the next day I was back in harness in the corn again. I slaved away as if they were going to pay me for a day's work with a bar of gold. I wanted lots of money, but I was also trying to forget the Zumbusch fiasco. My sweat washed it away, one drop at a time. The natives kept shaking their heads. I didn't strike them as being quite normal. They were also speaking such an abominable dialect that I didn't understand a quarter of what they were asking of me. And me they understood only about half the time.

"The *patrón* was a creole. He paid no attention to me. I didn't address a single word to him. Both the assignments and the pay were controlled by the foreman. He was also a creole, but this was a man with whom you could get along. At night the *capataz* and I would often sit in front of the big barn and tell each other a little about the capital. He had done military service there. He had picked up the usual nasty infection there, and the thing was now deeply seated in his kidneys. Sometimes he was overcome by colic out in the middle of a field. Then he would twist around on the ground like a snail whose shell has been stepped on. I would always stay with him for that quarter hour, until the stone had loosened itself and had slipped down into the bladder. This man had never been to see a doctor. He believed he could cure himself completely with tea. An old Indian woman collected the herbs for him: domestic horsetail, the leaves of red bilberries, the blossoms of bindweed, and thistle. He believed in that. He had been torturing himself that way for more than a decade, and the attacks were becoming more and more frequent. I only mention this *capataz* because he made those five weeks on the *chacra* bearable. Otherwise I'd have been another steer in the herd. When I took my leave I was wearing a magnificent *vicuña* poncho, red and yellow, and carrying two hundred and ten *pesos* in my pocket. I could have gotten another two weeks' work at the neighboring *estancia*. But by now I had really had enough of the camps. They don't give away anything here. Here society is still boarded shut. The ruler here is the man who owns the land. He makes the laws; the police are at his beck and call. He is the government, for it is his people who nominate the candidates who rule in his name. There is no difference between the *conquistadores* from Pizarro on down and the *caudillos* today. The flat land is sparsely inhabited. The population is composed of people of assorted nationalities. They come here to make money and not to go on strike. They don't sober up until they realize that all the gold was scratched out of the earth a long time ago. And that the earth is also full of weeds and vermin. And that they are there in order to transform the weeds and the vermin into wheat, corn, and herds of cattle and sheep.

"Those are the thoughts, my dear Julio, that occupy the mind on a train when it's speeding through a countryside where the fertile fields defy measurement. Thoughts that come when the earth screws itself with all its might into a man. When earth is no longer just a taste of dust on the tongue but something felt in the heart as a deep inhalation to which you don't know how to react. Because the rest of the things that clutter up our life won't relinquish any space. Because our life is packed full of things that don't belong there: piles of unnecessary debris and washed up antiquities.

"And after all, out there where there is nothing but the earth and what has grown out of it, the wind, the clouds, and the sun are also to be had; we weren't walking around out there with our eyes shut nor was mold growing in our ears. And our noses were still sensitive to different scents. It is certainly not crucial that anyone be able to distinguish accurately between the scent emanating from a wild camellia bush and that rising from a bromeliad's roots. He who does make the distinction has acquired the skill through practice. What does count though is that you have a sense of smell, period. That you have realized how deeply the grass can breathe after a rain. That you know what insanely vain qualities a tree can display in order to always turn its prettiest side to the sun. That you be aware that even the worms are trying to outsmart you; that they consider you dumb and that if things get rough for them, they spray you with their smelly excrement. The lagoon doesn't have just the one eye aimed up at the sky absorbing its color and revolving with its movement; the other eye is lurking below among the fish and roots and is full of poison, and bile, and an evil dragon when it's storming above. And when the sun shines again, there are the most succulent feasts among the herons and flamingos, the golden pheasants and the cormorants. Take a good look at the blue buzzard when he's up there perched on a cloud letting the wind hit him and splitting it in two: the cold stream for us and the warm one for the young in his nest high up on the outermost branch of a palm tree.

"We only experience all that when we are in a thoughtful state. When our hands are still; ... on one of those rare holidays they have. When we're not smoking or doing 'elbow bends' at the local bar. When we don't stick our nose into a newspaper and don't let our big mouth run over with useless diatribes about things that we don't understand and that don't concern us. I think it is only we who reflect on how little we know about what grows. The Indians live with nature. In the fields it's often impossible to distinguish them from a tree, from a rock, from a steer that has lain down to ruminate, from a pumpkin waiting to explode, or from a mountain lion preparing to pounce.

"Weighted down with thoughts like these, I actually should have turned back to where I had just come from. But as soon as the first outlying settlements of the city began to intrude on the horizon, all purposeful reflection quickly came to an end. The present was back and so were the questions: What will we eat tomorrow, and how will we pay for it? And how do we find a job and where? A job that pays enough to make us almost feel good about ourselves, thereby allowing us to rate God as a good guy after all. Finally the suburbs clattered by. Then well dressed people started to board. The girls had faces that seemed made of fine china; one even had red hair. And my thoughts immediately took me to Rosita. In these thoughts I was already mapping out where we'd go for dinner that night. Afterward, of course, on to a small hotel. Separated for eight weeks; that makes you store up a lot of tensions. The girls in the rail car were already cracking jokes about it. Rosita is one person to whom I won't be caught owing anything. Yessir, that much I resolved to do.

"I only noticed what I looked like when I was standing on the station's platform. It's certainly not a pretty sight when they catch you as you stumble in from the camps at corn harvest time. But I was even a sight more frazzled than most. I was forced to hail a taxi in order to reach my boarding house without creating a disturbance. That callous jerk of a taxi driver even demanded payment in advance. I held the wad of *pesos* under his nose and spat on his boots. And off we went.

"Zumbusch didn't cross my mind until I was on the stairs. Now there was someone with whom I certainly had a few accounts to settle. And when she opened the door, the landlady said to me: 'My God, ... Peter! You're supposed to be in Europe.'

"It took a good half hour for me to clear everything up for her and to explain that the corn fields in the camp where I was picking are situated not far from Santa Fe. Since when is Santa Fe Europe?

"And it took another half hour for me to realize that I no longer had lodgings here. That Zumbusch had long since picked up my things because I lay ill in the hospital and had to go to Europe.

"Tears were streaming down good Mrs. Schulze's face. But I was out my three suitcases. The sum of what they contained in the way of suits, underwear, valuables, and books came to a small fortune of around two thousand *pesos*. I took my head in my hands because I had the feeling that my temples were going to explode at any minute.

"Even today I really can't fathom how a feeling of peace finally came over me, a peace colder than ice. Two hundred and ten *pesos* in my pocket, rags for clothes, covered with grime, my three suitcases gone, no underwear, no ties, no suits. So first, let's find a bathtub. The icy feeling persisted. Another taxi ride. Fitted for a brand new set of shoes and apparel at *Gath y Chávez*. Gone were my two hundred and ten *pesos* as were another twenty my landlady had loaned me. But now I stood there again like a normal citizen of Buenos Aires, tucked and pressed in full compliance with all those silly rules of fashion. I was standing in Rosita's store and promptly addressed my salutations to her mother. Her reply was by no means an inducement to a hug. The ice got colder. And that was O.K., too. Otherwise I might not have held up while Mrs. Birnbaum finally said that I should know full well where Rosita was. And was I trying to pull something over on her? And if so, why? She was just an old woman. A long-suffering creature. She had sacrificed herself for this child.

"Then the same agonizing heaven-to-hell fall took place that I had seen before with my landlady. For Zumbusch had also stopped here to make a pickup. And of all things, it had been of Rosita. But not in my name. No. Rather, because I was a heel and wanted to stand Rosita up and head for Europe alone, it had been for himself. And from there straight to the justice of the peace. That had happened three weeks earlier. Precisely on the same day that a big red 'bird spider' had almost nipped me with its poisonous maw. Spiders have always brought me bad luck. There are three examples I can swear to. At night the spiders were there, and next day came the ill fortune. Interpret that in whatever way you will, I have experienced it when my thoughts were clear, and I believe in it: big spiders bring me bad luck.

"The landlady advanced me another fifty *pesos*. With these in hand I scoured the city one day after another for four long weeks. No one had the faintest notion concerning Zumbusch and Rosita. I combed all the travel agencies. None of the ships' passenger lists mentioned a thing about Zumbusch and Rosita. I became a nuisance at all the South American consulates with my dumb questions about Zumbusch and Rosita. No one knew anything about a visa. Whether I liked it or not, I was going to have to close the books on this case. I had to buy myself free from Zumbusch and Rosita in thought. Otherwise they'd have had to drag me off to the *manicomio*. And after all I still needed my head to stand behind a counter writing up advertisements: English, French, Spanish, for a hundred and twenty *pesos* a month. Here when you get such a high paying job, they call it hitting *la grande*. And the company's name was Lenglen. It went bankrupt just like Ellermann after four months. It was 'Black Friday' that finished it off.

"After five, six months Zumbusch was pretty well gone from my thoughts. Just not the redhead. The one named Rosita. Every Saturday afternoon at four I'd be sitting at Mrs. Birnbaum's having coffee with her. And we spoke of nothing else but Rosita.

"Exactly nine months had run their course when I read by chance in *La Crítica* of a band of criminals that had shipped scores of women illegally to Chile, to Peru, to Montevideo, and to the provinces. This was nothing new at the time. You would read about it nearly every day in the newspaper as you would about soccer, and about the horse races, about Tranquilino Vallejos, the *gaucho*, about Carlos Gardel, about the Virgencita de Madera, about a revolution in Ecuador, about locusts and about – Oh God, Oh God! – about how wheat prices have fallen again.

"But of the five gang members who were named one was called Zumbusch. Here this is no common, everyday name; it could only turn up once.

"So I took a day's leave and checked with the police; an acquaintance of mine worked down there. And that facilitated my entry into the *calabozo* to which Zumbusch had been assigned. I went into no further theatrics with him; I only wanted to know where to find Rosita. When ten minutes had gone by and I had promised to get him an attorney as well as to leave him ten *pesos* cash, he said to me that Rosita was being well kept in an elegant house in Montevideo. No gentleman was admitted there for less than ten *pesos*.

"That was my reunion with Zumbusch, after which he also explained – upon his honor and as God was his witness! – that the whole incident probably would not have happened if I had not fallen into such an incredibly deep sleep and been impossible to wake up in Córdoba. I alone was to blame for the whole disaster. Especially for his present incarceration. And for Rosita being in Montevideo. If I were not to find him a competent lawyer, he'd have no other recourse but to hang himself. Then I'd really have my just reward.

"I did not give him the beating he deserved for these impertinent remarks although no one would have stopped me; quite the contrary. But he appeared so beaten up that a first rate surgeon should have been called in.

"My police acquaintance, who had witnessed the entire conversation with Zumbusch, told me afterwards: 'My dear friend, do not hire a lawyer for this seller of souls; you could end up working five years just to pay off his crooked counselor.'

"But I went ahead and hired Zumbusch a lawyer anyway. And the lawyer was able to negotiate a reduction of one and a half years on the two year sentence given Zumbusch by the judge. He didn't take a single *centavo* from me. In fact this lawyer was not one of the slick local cutthroats; he was of German parentage. I was supposed to recommend him to others. Which I am herewith doing. I don't want to waste any more breath on Rosita. After a year of the most feverish kind of work she switched over to a less pricey establishment. Clearly that type of ladder is one that always takes you downward, ever deeper and deeper...."

"Well ... ," said Don Julio, as he ran his fingers through his hair. "The pill you've had to swallow has certainly been bitter enough!"

Chapter Fourteen

Johann Peter Langfoot was tired of letting so-called circumstances make matters worse in what pertained to his life; the figure he cut was shaping up badly enough as things stood. The world that lay before him seemed to him gray and worm-eaten like a superannuated cheese. The stench no longer mattered in the least. That much his nose could ignore. But the sensitivity of the organ called soul could not follow suit. No one knows where the soul resides, whether tucked away up in some inner recess of the brain or as an invisible gas all around us. In any case every one of us thinks he has one. Why shouldn't he too have a soul? Indeed he possessed one to a considerable degree. He suffered from it though no one wanted to take his word for it. To be sure he didn't place that much value on such a belief. Instead, for the past several weeks he had placed more value on disappearing somewhere and being forgotten. He didn't expect that from the jungle any more, now that jungles no longer existed as white specks on maps. And so he continued on his way as an insignificant 'ordinary' man. The absurdity of life is bound to come to an end somewhere. Though his soul was gathering around his ego in an attitude of deep suffering, he no longer paid its mute warnings any heed. As a result he was getting splitting headaches. They began at the back of the head, settled for a while in his ears, then descended through the neck vertebra. Walking turned into a difficult problem for him. But it was a problem he wanted to solve at all costs in order to arrive at his goal.

Slowly he walked down *Calle Garay*. Over the years he had sauntered, and sometimes also run, hundreds of times down this not unclean street. He found that certain house too where for three *pesos* he had now and then dared to have a little fling. He went into the familiar house on this occasion as well, opened his chest pouch in the downstairs hall, and found that he still had thirteen *pesos* left to live on. A long, narrow courtyard yet remained to be crossed. In passing, he heard a loudspeaker blaring: "Revolution in Cuba! The *revolucionarios* are firing cannons at the banks and hospitals from a ship offshore. Schools and the Museum of Fine Arts in ashes. The *revolucionarios* are aiming their machine guns at the Governor's Palace. Above the palm trees, the tobacco and sugarcane plantations whipped by ocean winds...."

There was crackling and spluttering. The revolution in the loudspeaker seemed over. It was Carlos Gardel's turn to speak, make that sing, again. He was singing the tango '*Pan y agua*.' The entire population of the neighboring brothels was singing '*Pan y agua*.' Johann Peter Langfoot had had enough for a while. He walked up the three steps with which he was so familiar and rang the bell.

The same two old gals were still minding the store: Carmen and Louicia. He sat down on the bed next to Louicia and told her that he had to take a trip that would last a considerably long time. Surely one could take along a bite for the road. He'd prefer the kind that people haven't yet managed to drag around with them in tubes or cans. "In the next thirty to fifty years that will probably be available too. And as soon as it happens, your business, like so many others before it, will also be wiped out. Me ... , I still want to stuff a quick couple of *pesos* into your stocking. I see you've gotten a little thinner. But as you well know, the spot that is still the most sensitive is behind my left ear. Please don't forget that."

She waited on him quite decently. She even allowed a little snippet of her inner self to escape. Afterwards they drank *mate* together because business was not going well at the moment. The word must have gotten out about the revolution in Cuba. "Anyway Pedrito my sweet, do you know that I'll soon be calling it quits in this establishment and taking over a stationery shop on the *Calle México*. You know, ... right across from the church? They sell about thirty religious pictures a day over there not to mention the votive candles. That's a clean profit of twenty *pesos* anyway. Notebooks and pencils and pens make another two. If I want to make that kind of money here, why I have to take a lot of guff and overexert myself. Because half of what we collect for taking guff and exerting ourselves is, of course, the landlady's. What's the matter with you, my dear? Today you're not in good form at all. You haven't caught yourself a cold now, have you? Or has your grandmother gone and died on you? Why, word has it that just this past week a bunch of people died of the flu. You just watch yourself! Saturnio Bosso, who usually came by every Wednesday and Saturday, hasn't shown his face here in two weeks. I already believed that he had become unfaithful to me. But in reality he wasn't actually that naughty. Chacarita Cemetery has taken him into her bosom. Row VIII, grave number 2407. His wife goes there every afternoon and cries. I should do that too. But after all the business isn't taking in that much. And he didn't leave me anything in his will either. Maybe he did, but his wife prefers to save it for the three little ones.

"Nope ... , I just can't seem to get much of anything going with you today. Otherwise I'd suggest an encore to soften the trauma of separation. When you come back next time – assuming this trip of yours doesn't go to the ends of the earth – then I'll demonstrate something entirely new for you.

"I mean, there's no real hurry for me to get into the stationery business. Besides, I still lack two hundred *pesos* for the down payment. It'll take more than two weeks for those to trickle in. So I hope you fare well and even better, my dear one and only. Let your trip be a good one and may we meet again."

Louicia even went so far as to lean out the window; the white flesh of her bosom came loose. Her last and no doubt most original farewell gesture. Johann Peter took it with him as he would the scent of a special perfume. Nevertheless he spat to one side, then mumbled to himself: "So that's what the last meal tastes like the night before the execution."

The road ahead of him was anything but straight. He hadn't even intended to look up old Lezama Park, a favorite place of his. But now it stood before him and made the blackness before his eyes even darker. He stopped to rest a little on the old familiar bench beneath the four-hundred-year-old magnolia tree. An incredibly old owl was hacking away miserably in the upper branches. Langfoot covered both his ears. He remembered that even as a boy he was afraid of an owl's screech. Sleep was seeping into his eyes. It took all his strength to keep them wide open. A fat mustachioed policemen was suddenly probing all over his face with a flashlight. The man actually dared to rouse him with a good piece of advice: frankly it was too cold today to spend the night on a bench; as if Johann Peter had ever had that intention.

Freezing chills ran up and down his back as he rose to his feet again. He staggered downhill. The street down which he was stumbling like this was no longer familiar to him. He could only see that he was approaching the water again. Ramshackle tin huts and the sickening smell of half-rotten human offal. Vermin and poverty such that it can't be helped by conventional means because it does not grasp that it is an absolutely useless poverty. Accordions and bawdy songs are there to seal the emotions yet deeper in their coffin, down among the women's stifled voices and the cancer riddled wombs.

Under the last street lamp lay a drunken sailor relieved of his belongings down to his shirt. He was throwing up his guts and screaming periodically for his mother. Possibly a young greenhorn (from Oslo judging by his speech), who had never been sent on a trip this far from home before.

Today everything went right over Johann Peter Langfoot without eliciting any emotion, for, God knows, he had already experienced it umpteen times before. He had often stood atop the refuse heap of our society in the past and been thoroughly nauseated by the repugnance of this miserable world.

Johann Peter walked across a bridge. The black shapes of several ships were rocking on even darker water. Bubbles of air were gurgling up from the bottom and bursting with an oily stench.

On the western horizon quite low already Sirius stood out like a blue diamond. A few stories higher the moon was orbiting in the company of a threatening red retinue.

Johann Peter was already giving himself a shove to turn his back on this life once and for all. He hit his forehead against a rail section that he had not noticed in the dark. His birds woke up and started making noise. He clearly heard the word "shiiit!" At last his misfortunate birds were making a sensible statement again.

"If this is shiiit, then go for it!" he answered and rubbed his forehead. A huge lump was growing out of it like a horn. "Well how about that!" he said to himself and made an about-face on the spot. Now he had the Southern Cross before him again as well as the long, endless body of the 'great Hydra.' He followed this constellation and ended up where half a *peso* gets you a warm bowl of soup and a place to sleep. The bedbugs walked right over his face into his dream. The dream suddenly broke off. The triangular stiletto of a black-skinned senior bedbug was boring its way into his left breast and using the opportunity to take control of the chest pouch. The broken piece of steel was stuck where it had entered. The chest pouch pulled out together with the other part of the knife. It was an unconscious man that the attendants of the nearby hospital put on a stretcher.

"A German?" asked the doctor on the night shift.

"That's right, a *boche*!" answered the receptionist.

"Oh, then nothing much will go wrong. Those people have savage survival instincts."

It was seven weeks to the day and hour that Johann Peter Langfoot had lain in the hospital. They had carded his stomach and brushed his lungs clean. They had opened his pericardium and sewn it shut again. Iodine in a metallic shade of brown glistened on his body from throat to testicles. Cooking salt and epinephrine stood ready for any eventuality. His breathing was sporadic. Two and a half liters of oxygen were held in reserve and, just in case, four ampoules of camphor. A blood transfusion was necessary! When it was all over, a man lay there who no longer consisted of anything but brain. He woke up much too early. He saw the steam rising from the sterilizers. He saw Nurse Angelika and Nurse Maddalena. On the glass trays he saw the tweezers and the clamps, the hooks and the forceps. There were needles, both straight and curved, and threads of silk and catgut on sparkling porcelain spools. He yanked his arm out of the leather sling and delivered quite an artful punch to the aide's chin. Five days later they were strapping him down again; they had forgotten a pair of scissors in his stomach. They took advantage of this once-in-a-lifetime opportunity to excise a fistula from one of his nasal cavities, and then they brushed blood back into his veins again. What a brave man! A puma turned lamb, yet without the strength to spit blood or bile. He only spat water and the contents of his bowels into the bucket that stood ready. By the time three weeks had gone by he was already asking for a strong pea soup with ham; and after another three, he was asking for an evening pass to visit a brothel.

In the interim the nurses had allowed him to grow a full beard and had pulled the clumps of hair out of his ears. They had seen his genitalia many times and had come to the realization that his mouth, which was often terribly contorted by pain and twisted beyond recognition, still remained a nest full of oaths. It was only the birds, about which he had fantasized after the last ceremonial carnage, that the professors could not locate in his skull. Just a small undulation on cranial ridge number twenty-four. "Years down the road it'll wear off! It'll wear off, Langfoot my friend."

After that he hit on the idea of asking the nurses for a mirror. They brought him an elegant monstrosity. On looking into it, he found that in appearance he could now be mistaken for his grandfather August. Grandfather August died in his ninety-third year after remarrying in his sixty-eighth.

"Not a bad sign at all, this mirror image," thought Langfoot to himself. "Going by that, quite a lot still lies ahead of me." And now he'd gladly also have said something nice and endearing to Nurse Enriqueta. But they had no sense of humor here where the house rules were concerned, and a few of the nurses strictly abided by the even stricter regulations; in other words they abided by only those rules intended for third class patients.

Nearly every day some poor devil died in a bed close by, and the family would conduct an elaborate funeral. The latest to die was *señor* Atripaldo Tabacho, a resident of *Calle Brasil*. He was the owner of a successful flower and wreath shop and of a bleach-blond wife named Atalanta. Once she had recognized Johann Peter Langfoot as that which her husband could no longer be, she also turned her thoughts to him whenever she paid the prescribed visits to her husband. She had a lot of friendly looks to spare for him. She brought along butter cookies for him even though he wasn't hungry. She brought him navel oranges although he was only supposed to sip chicken broth. She brought him an edition of *Don Quixote,* and he read it once and then again. Everything hung heavy on his mind. It was all being stored in his brain yet nothing sensible would come out. After piously lending her ear to his complaints, *señora* Atalanta was finally of the opinion that it would be much nicer if he were to recuperate, leave the premises for good, and settle in at her place while in transition. They would soon arrive at an agreement concerning the price of the separate room with bath and telephone, board, and all sorts of other amenities. "Because this time, of course, it's not only about making a profit from the boarder."

When Johann Peter appeared at *señora* Atalanta's door, *señor* Atripaldo Tabacho had already lain underground some two weeks. Under a mammoth pile of wilted flowers. Under a snow white marble obelisk with gold lettering. Under the weekly Sunday visit of *señora* Atalanta. Under the telltale sigh that Johann Peter Langfoot heaved when he first saw the pretentious mound of dirt piled on top of the man who had lain next to him for five weeks.

Señora Atalanta didn't say no when Langfoot formally announced that he would be stopping by and was there immediately. His papers were in order so far. After only one hour of pleasant conversation, *señora* Atalanta gave him an introductory kiss, which had an appropriate taste of garlic and rotten meat. However when she opened her drawers, threw herself on the bed before the bedspread had even been pulled down, and lifted up her thighs, he laughed out loud at the lascivious directness of the female sex.

Atalanta was so startled by this that she crossed herself without even changing position.

What had prompted Johann Peter to explode into such uncontrolled laughter is something *señora* Atalanta will never find out. Nor will the esteemed gentleman reader; perhaps not even the no less esteemed female reader has the hope of ever understanding, unless assisted by psychic deep sea divers. We should never carry our curiosity to extremes concerning the outcome of cases, like the present one, that don't set a good example. Suffice it to say here that once Johann Peter had laughed himself out, he grabbed his cap and strode into the street without looking back again.

Johann Peter was taken in by a friendly *boliche,* smoke-cured both inside and out. Food? The very thought nauseated him. A sip of strong schnaps? The head doctor had forbidden him that for at least six weeks during the talk he was given at the time of his release. A cup of java? That was the right choice at last. He drank three cups of coffee one right after the other. Only then did it get quiet among his thoughts. And so he told himself: By God, Peterman old boy, you're on the road to recovery! It's the first time you've shown restraint where otherwise no one else can. What's wrong with you?

"Waiter! A double *caña*! A green one. Cuban."

"Yes, indeed. *Caña*! Now more than ever. This is probably the same dear comforter that Isaiah meant, "Then the eyes of the blind shall be opened and the ransomed of the Lord shall return...."

He looked down and saw the fly on his trousers gaping wide open. He buttoned the darkness back up again in which Atalanta had wished to shed light.

Behind him he heard a woman's voice whisper, "No, in times like these no children should come into the world!" It came from the garishly painted mouth of a mulatto woman and was intended for a much fairer adolescent boy. What this pimply teenager responded remained unintelligible to Johann Peter. Too bad, he mumbled to himself. When a female of the species finally utters a reasonable question via her intrinsically gorgeous chops, it ends up being a foolish emissary of civilization who gets away with the answer. I can't deny, however, that I replied with appropriate laughter when a mere object was prompting me to answer. The woman for whom the laughter was intended understood me better than she did the man who was so offended by such antics that he allowed himself to be buried in this place because with his ravaged brain he could no longer answer any questions, let alone ask them.

So I have become an obedient little dog after all, even though I never in my dreams thought that I'd be living according to the sound advice of those medical gentlemen, that is, giving up the joys of female companionship for a year. Actually wasn't I always left joyless, even with my first love, who for no reason died and left me? Is it even possible ever to be happy with a woman? Why does a woman want it, though? Sadly, Peter old buddy, she too only experiences happiness once and never again. Afterwards she too suffers for the rest of her life from personal loneliness. No drunkenness helps get over it, no intimacy in a drunken state.

He was the last one to leave the establishment. A bench in the waiting room of the southside train station took him in. Lying on the bench at exactly six o'clock the next morning, he felt someone shaking him awake. An unkempt goatee was grinning at him: "If you have no lice and desire to work, you can start up at my place. I pay five *pesos*. You have no other responsibility than to pour a gray purée into tin cans. I'm the one who whips up the mash. You don't need to rack your brain about the ingredients. My patent answers for that. I make a suitable profit. I can tell by the tip of your nose that you're a veteran. Veterans are my favorite co-workers. A corporal has sealed your mouth for all time."

"*Bueno*," said Johann Peter, "if the work will keep, you can expect me this evening after closing time. Where is your worthy establishment located?"

"Chiclana 7350. I am the one who puts out the watchdog."

"Understood. Now I'm on my way to have breakfast, and while I'm at it, I'd prefer not to be disturbed."

As Johann Peter made his way to the old *lechería* that he had become so fond of in hard times, he carried his personal satisfaction around like a flower smelling of Russian leather. Forgotten was Atalanta. And what she had uncovered no less so. He found himself in a state that was the exact opposite of that which had moved him upon entering Atalanta's apartment.

After ordering hot milk in the dairy shop and while the milk cooled off and developed a thick skin, he reflected once more on the intermezzo with Atalanta that had unfolded in such a funny way. He focused especially on the laughter. From what depths had it emerged? In him who had always held to the belief that laughter is nothing more than the revenge of the unfree individual? Have I, who always considered myself to be the Eternal German, suddenly become so unfree? Then I'm also entitled to reassume my bondage by signing up as someone's peon. As he came to this half-mumbled realization, Langfoot's heart was hammering time into a thin bit of nothing, and presently there was no reason at hand to hope for better times as an enlisted man. So it was bound to happen that he should turn up three hours sooner than agreed at the unkempt goatee's place of business to receive his pay in lump form.

"Why such trust? You don't even know whether I'll be back."

"A person couldn't size you up to be any dumber than what can be read on your face."

"You have pronounced the magic word, and therefore you will be rewarded. I'll be here!"

An hour later he got lucky with the cash because fate would have it that the mulatto woman who had resolved not to bring any children into the world crossed his path again.

When she asked him, "What for? You don't even know if I'm available." He answered, "Because I assuredly am, and still don't want to."

He wiped the insulted woman's spittle off his face without saying a word and went looking for a hole in which to sleep. A cheerful soap maker provided just the place. It cost ten *pesos* a week. The narrow, crooked rungs going up like a chicken ladder had been polished till they gleamed.

Chapter Fifteen

Blue-black clusters of clouds were climbing up out of the ocean, crossing the wide river, climbing higher and higher, and driving a dirty green darkness along in front of them. It was quicker than the rain. The contours of all salient objects became blurred. The skyscrapers looked like heaps of slag now. A sulfurous heat was pouring out of their windows. Thunder rolled in the distance.

Johann Peter Langfoot was sitting at the open window of his small garret. He had not wanted to occupy the room on the ground level that was offered to him first. He felt that it was much too large for a single person who would only spend a few hours there. Then they showed him the garret — which until then had served as a storeroom — and those quarters suited him very nicely. "Now it resembles the cloistered cell of a spinster," he said to Timm, who had come back onto the scene and had helped him arrange his things. "And that's how I'll have to perceive myself in the future. Because I swear I've resolved to be serious and to start behaving myself."

He had been staying with the Langmanns for seven weeks now, and he had been liking it more and more with each passing day.

Today he was free for the day again and sporting a clean shave as well. Basically his intention was to make a trip into town and borrow a couple of books from his friend the book dealer. There was a new novel out by Silone. He hadn't read anything by Silone yet. But he also felt like getting his hands on *Nachsommer* by Stifter and on Fontane's *Der Stechlin* again.

Now the approaching storm was crossing his path. And turbulence that comes out of that windy corner is really violent. It often requires twenty-four hours to blow over.

This led Johann Peter Langfoot to seriously consider whether the lower middle class lifestyle he was leading in this house represented the last episode in the evolution of his earthly existence or whether he should only view it as a restful pause. He resolved to talk with Timm about it. And these complicated issues really deserved to be discussed with the Langmanns as well. It needn't be today, of course, but soon and at an opportune moment.

There were three adults in the household: Otto Langmann and his wife Martha as well as Hans-Heinrich, Otto's older, widowed brother. In addition three children were part of the family; two of them were boys aged nine and eleven who were Otto's pride and joy, and there was the thirteen-year-old girl, Marie-Louise, who was Hans-Heinrich's daughter.

The two Langmanns had been in Argentina for over thirty years now. They set foot on Argentine soil when they were children but had not blended in at all. A large manufacturer in Plauen had sent their father to Buenos Aires to set up a stocking factory. He had then become the technical director of the plant and had taken his two sons into the business. The old man had died ten years ago; his wife had followed him one year later. She did not want to be laid to rest in this 'barbaric foreign soil here,' however, and consequently the ashes of both parents were transported to Germany and deposited in a cinerarium near Dresden. Hans-Heinrich had seen to their transportation. When he returned to Argentina, his young wife already lay underground.

What his sons had inherited from old Mr. Langmann was not a large fortune. As a 'good German patriot' he had thought it his duty to invest almost all the available cash in war bonds. And it's common knowledge that as an investment these did not pan out. Yet there were enough savings left for the Langmanns to build this nice house in the suburb of Olivos. The property included another healthy parcel of land with no construction on it. That was intended for Hans-Heinrich, the brother, in case he decided to remarry. But he still didn't feel like doing it. He and his dead wife had had an outstanding marriage. His love for her was the kind which few women ever have the luck to know: it was a pure love, and one that was meant to last. Unfortunately when measured in years it hadn't lasted but a short time. Even now, Hans-Heinrich could still not grasp that this woman was no longer present. Yet it wasn't easily apparent to others. Strictly to look at him, he appeared to live here as in his own home. His little girl was excellently provided for. Aunt Martha did a perfect job of standing in for her mother. And Johann Peter felt a deep, quiet love for the child, spending hours in conversation with her when it was his day off and he was at the house.

One day, after a brotherly friendship had developed between them, Johann Peter said to Otto Langmann: "I've heard that the factory is supposed to pass into American hands as a precaution, so to speak, because we all know there is so much uncertainty in the air. And if this proves accurate … , then in all likelihood you folks will have to relocate since deep down you still aren't Argentineans at heart."

"This business about selling the factory to some Americans is one of many speculative rumors that are too transparent to be taken seriously. No, we'll remain what we are. We are completely independent.

"But I'd also like to tell you something else, Peter. For several weeks now I've been working on arranging a position for you at the plant. It's just that the right position for you had not opened up until now. You could easily have been hired for the warehouse right from the start. But the thirty *Taler* a week salary which is disbursed by the firm didn't sit well with us. What would you say to being hired as a dispatcher? To begin with you would clear one hundred and eighty *pesos* monthly; then in six months, after you had learned the ropes well, you could count on two hundred and fifty *pesos*. Would you be interested?"

"There's no question that the desire is there, Otto. The other more urgent question is whether this old bag of bones, complete with his head full of ne'er-do-well birds, will be suitable for the job. I don't wish to accept charity, and above all I don't want to create any problems for you and your brother. What will be required of me at this job, anyway? I mean aside from reading, writing, and arithmetic?"

"Compared to what you're capable of doing, Peter, not much! We can certainly trust you with a simple inventory ledger, can't we? And you're not color-blind either. For the rest everything will depend on keeping a sharp eye on the fingers of the girls in the stock room. Every business has its share of thievery. But silk stockings are something that is inordinately attractive ... , especially to eyes and fingers that aren't necessarily adhesive to begin with. Time had caused your predecessor to lose his eye for that. Or else there were other reasons for his blindness. When you're dealing with the local girls, there are times when kidding around is not all you do. A few of them have fiendish pudenda."

"*Bueno*," answered Johann Peter, "if the three of you want to give me a try ... , I have nothing against it. In the event things don't work out, we are by no means forced to break off our friendship. As you know, I am not the hypersensitive type nor have I ever been. And every first step is always the hardest, isn't it?"

"The second dispatcher, who is the son of some friends of ours, will be at your side training you, so to speak, but don't let that concern you because the fellow is barely twenty-one. Otherwise a fine, upstanding young man although a shade too introverted for someone his age, if you ask me. He has heard of you, by the way."

"If the youngster is otherwise agreeable, I'm sure we'll get along together. I have always enjoyed the company of young people and not just that of the female variety either. In this country the young people have seldom become my friends though."

"I'm really glad that you've accepted my offer. Believe me, we often worried about your welfare. Do you want to start next Monday? I would certainly like that. Or could it be they won't release you from your present job right away?"

"The day the boss gets tired of looking at my face he can throw me back out on the street immediately. Therefore I must also be justified in vacating my position in the interest of some other poor devil. He gets ten for every one. And I may safely say that by some miracle, with no effort on my part, I slipped a few steps up in the world by way of a chicken ladder."

"It's not that I'm trying to be critical when I say that you might have found another more substantial job than to throw yourself head first into peonage, Peter. Just what made you do it, anyway?"

Johann Peter raised his eyes to the ceiling and felt a cold shudder go up his back. He succeeded in shaking off the attack though and said: "At a time when I stood at the ultimate brink of all the brinks of this bottomless precipice, it seemed to me that scrounging around out there among the exalted gentry, regardless of persuasion, in hopes that they would put in a good word for me was the equivalent of going on pilgrimage to a relic known for its miraculous powers. You may not understand the comparison right away, Otto, but it's accurate. And the reason for its accuracy is something I'll tell you if after I have spent four weeks with your firm you say to me: 'Peter, you've made a decent effort at it, but unfortunately you're not suited to dry work like this. Your best bet is to try and land a job wearing a general's uniform as the bouncer in a fancy juice joint!' Should you, on the other hand, be somehow better satisfied with my work, then a body could regain the hope that all is not yet lost for old Peter despite the continued chirping of his birds."

"This is a side of you that we're getting to know for the very first time," laughed Otto Langmann. "All I can tell you is that putting you on this job doesn't worry me in the least. And while I have this opportunity, I'd also like to invite you to eat with us if you like. Where six people can eat their fill, the seventh surely won't be left wanting. More than once now our children have asked: 'Why is it that uncle Peter doesn't sit at the table with us? It's obvious he's always alone and maybe he can't get enough to eat....' To be sure, out of the mouths of babes there always comes the truth. You also share that opinion, don't you? Consequently I hope that you'll consent to be the seventh member of our family as of next Sunday."

"Fine, Otto ... , I'm happy to say yes when it's not a matter of charity. Everyone knows that not even death is for free. So I'll discuss the financial aspect of this deal with your wife; then we're sure to find the proper way for our journey together to be successful."

In the days that followed Johann Peter felt rather miserable and ill at ease. He wasn't absolutely certain yet whether he wanted to accept the position at the textile mill or not. It wasn't the work itself that frightened him. If they were not asking anything more of him than that he supervise shipments and deliveries and keep an eye on the sticky fingers of the girls in the stock room … , it certainly doesn't take a genius to pull that off. But then comes dependency on the Langmanns. Always asking yourself what else you need to do to demonstrate the gratitude owed to your friends?! Naturally to be grateful in this case ends up being a goddamn duty and obligation. I'd be a scoundrel if I chose to cop out on it.

Given the condition he was in, it was lucky that for a while the new job at the factory absorbed him completely. There were a hundred and fourteen shades of brown in this year's collection of ladies' pure silk hosiery. This was something that had to be stringently memorized. One hundred and fourteen shades of brown! At first he could barely distinguish thirty. "Tomorrow you're bound to hit fifty," said the assistant soothingly, who was doing everything he could to 'train' Johann Peter.

Johann Peter grumbled, "And in another year there will be nine hundred and ninety-nine shades of brown. Why, of all things, does it have to be this offensive brown color? I favor black; it's better attuned to the dark events of our time."

Silently he thought on: I'm still going through the same experience as the guy who doesn't understand anything about fashion but nevertheless has to pay. So tomorrow I'm supposed to understand the meaning of fashion and how you sell people on it while simultaneously getting paid to do so. A human being simply has to be a magician, not just a chameleon! Otherwise he's nothing more than a damned s.o.b. In the few years I've spent here I have had to expend more in the way of nervous energy than in my eighteen years of practical apprenticeship. It won't be long before I'll find myself patting myself on the back and alternately burying my nose in either my song book or my check book.

It was on this windy, rainy day that Johann Peter had successfully come through his trial period. For lunch there was baked rabbit with potato dumplings on the side. There was a rich pale wine from Mendoza, almost a chablis, and a small, fine Havana cigar. Now that's the style of the Langmanns!

Presently on seeing Marie-Louise's hands and then touching them while being congratulated, he found that they were no longer the same hands to which his thoughts had wandered that morning. The eyes fit, though, and so did the hair. The mouth was a bit too youthful yet. The mouth had a wish. After dinner the wish was stated out loud: "On Sunday afternoon, uncle Peter, we'll go to the movies, won't we?"

Glossary

Ahasuerus: the Wandering Jew, a legendary character doomed to live until the end of the world since he taunted Jesus on the way to the crucifixion.

almacén: shop.

almacenero: shopkeeper.

altiplano: altiplanicie or high plateau, a great interior drainage basin for the Cordillera, especially in Bolivia.

Apiahy: Apiau, a Brazilian river.

ara: a genus of South American macaws.

Asunción: capital of Paraguay.

barranca: ravine, gorge, canyon.

boche: a French pejorative term for "German."

Bochum: a German industrial city located in the Ruhr.

boliche: tavern.

bombachas: baggy trousers.

bombilla: straw for sipping (mate).

Bromberg and Pillkallen: towns in what was formerly East and West Prussia, here: "in the sticks."

bromelia: a genus of tropical plants commonly growing on trees or rocks and remarkable for the hardness and dryness of their grey foliage.

bromural: sedative, tranquilizer.

Bukovina: a region including the northeastern Carpathian mountains and plains, belonging in part to present day Rumania.

calabozo: jail, dungeon

calle: street.

caña: distilled liquor made from sugar cane.

capatáz: foreman.

Carlos Gardel: well-known tango singer idolized after his untimely death in 1935.

caudillo: renegade land holder, outlaw, ring leader.

Chacarita: a major cemetery in Buenos Aires.

chacra: farm.

colectivo: bus.

comisaría: police station.

Cordillera: the Andes in South America and also their extension into Mexico and the North.

Córdoba: like-named city and province north and west of the province of Buenos Aires.

Corrientes: city in eastern province of same name, bordering Paraguay and Brazil.

criolla, criollo: Creole, native of mixed blood.

Deborah: Biblical prophetess and judge of Israel.

Deutscher Klub: German Club.

espinillo: South American tree of moderate height.

estancia: ranch.

estanciero: owner or foreman of a ranch.

feria: outdoor market, fair.

Flores: Las Flores, village located south and west of the city of Buenos Aires.

Fontane: Theodor Fontane, 1819-1898, German poet, novelist, essayist. The novel *Der Stechlin* (Stechlin) dates from 1899.

gallnut: gall apple, especially the nut or gall of the gall oak.

galpón: shack.

gobernación: government.

Gran Chaco: region in the interior of South America encompassing territory in northern Argentina, eastern Bolivia, western Brazil, and Paraguay.

guanaco: a wooly, reddish-brown animal of the Andes, related to the camel but without the humps.

Guaraní: a group of South American Indian tribes as well as their language, widely spoken in modern Paraguay.

hierba, yerba: grass, herb.

Iguassú: Brazilian river and famous waterfall.

Johann Wolfgang: a reference to Johann Wolfgang von Goethe (1749-1832), Germany's foremost author, best known for *Faust I* (1808).

Jujuy: a northern province of Argentina bordering on Bolivia.

Kohlhaasenbrück: town on the banks of the Havel river inhabited by the central figure in Heinrich von Kleist's novella *Michael Kohlhaas* (1810).

Landsmann: fellow countryman.

lechería: dairy store.

lechero: milk vendor.

lyngheras: tramps.

Mach's gut!: Take care!

maní: peanuts.

manicomio: insane asylum.

Manzanillo: Cuban port city, here a Cuban cigar.

mate: South American gourd or beverage sipped therefrom (see yerba below).

Mendoza: a province and city in Argentina known for wines production.

Michaelmas: the feast of St. Michael, the archangel, celebrated on the twenty-ninth of September.

mimosa: any of a large genus of trees, shrubs, and herbs native to warm regions and often with prickly leaves.

muermo: a Chilean tree of the rose family.

ñandú: nandu, the South American ostrich.

paciencia: patience.

panicle: loose, irregularly arranged flower cluster.

Paraná: a major river, which with its tributaries flows from central Brazil to the estuary of the Rio de la Plata at Buenos Aires.

patrón: boss.

pisco: a muscat brandy.

poco a poco: little by little.

Pompeya: a suburb of Buenos Aires or small town on its outskirts, apparently fictitious.

puchero: an everyday stewlike dish.

quebracho: an Argentinean hardwood tree, the bark and wood of which is variously used in medicine, tanning, and dyeing.

Quechua: Quichua, an Indian people originally of Peru.

Reconquista: the reconquest of Spain and end of Moorish domination.

Rinaldo Rinaldini: a bandit celebrated since the eighteenth century in the popular imagination as the foe of tyranny and protector of the oppressed; the title of a three-volume work (1798) by Christian Vulpius.

Rindsbraten: roast beef.

Saint Anthony: ca. 250-350, the first Christian monk, described by one source as "the pioneer of desert monasticism"; he was the subject of legends recording the temptations that beset him. His help is sought to find lost objects.

Saint Hieronymus: 340?-420, Church father, published the Latin version of the Bible, the Vulgate.

San Juan: city in Argentina and capital of the province by the same name.

Schlemihl: the central figure of the novella *Peter Schlemihls wundersame Geschichte* (Peter Schlemihl's Strange Story, 1814) by Adelbert von Chamisso (1781-1836), which relates how he bartered away his shadow and therefore was fated to spend his life roaming the world; also a Yiddish term for an inefficient bungling person who habitually fails or is easily victimized.

Schweinebraten: German-style roast pork.

Shantung: eastern province of China.

Siebenbürgen: Transylvania, a region belonging to Rumania since World War I.

Silone: Ignazio Silone, Italian anti-Fascist author, born in 1900; he spent the war years in exile in Switzerland.

Stifter: Adalbert Stifter, 1805-1868, an Austrian narrative writer characterized as a poetic realist. His novel *Der Nachsommer* (Indian Summer) from 1857 is in the tradition of the *Bildungsroman*.

tacurú: ant mound; also small Argentinean ant.

Taler: a monetary unit dating from the sixteenth century prevalent in parts of Germany; here the term is used generically for *peso*.

tanagra: Tanagra, tanager. Colorful New World bird of the Thraupidae family.

Terrabussa: a colony of German settlers inhabiting a valley 200 km. south of San Juan, possibly fictitious.

Tierra del Fuego: an archipelago at the southern extremity of South America.

Tranquilino Vallejos: a minor entertainer, possibly fictitious.

tranvía: streetcar.

tren de carga: freight train.

Trollhättän: city in southern Sweden.

Vergil: Virgil, 70-19 B.C., Roman poet best known as author of *The Aeneid*.

vicuña: South American animal related to the llama and alpaca, of the camel family.

Virgencita de Madera: the little wooden virgin.

yacaré: yacare or jacare, a Brazilian alligator.

yerba: a plant or herb, usually yerba mate, Paraguay tea.

Translator's Note

Paul Zech and I have a rare experience in common: forces beyond our control obliged each of us to leave familiar surroundings and begin our lives over again on another continent, in a different language, and under what we each perceived to be inhospitable circumstances. We are different in that I was still an adolescent when I left the U.S. for Germany with my parents in the fifties. Zech, on the other hand, was middle-aged.

To pull up stakes and relocate in a foreign country is seldom a painless process. I speak from personal experience; I am the daughter of a diplomat. Yet the younger we are, the better we seem to adapt to new surroundings.

When I read *Die Vögel des Herrn Langfoot* in Zech's original German, I found it easy, in light of my own experiences, to identify with Langfoot's alienation. He is, in my view, the misfit persona of his unhappily exiled creator. Even more helpful in relating to the protagonist was the fact that I had made a comparable journey to Argentina, where the novel is set, shortly before Ward Lewis and Camden House invited me to do this translation.

Fortunately, both Johann Peter Langfoot and I eventually made happy landings. However, the means and the mindset that led us there differ enormously. As the reader thumbs through the chapters of Langfoot's escapades, he will encounter vulgarity juxtaposed with pedantry, inhuman cruelty offset by soaring lyricism, and bigotry assailed while simultaneously being practiced. These passages express a resentment felt not only by Zech and Langfoot, but often by countless other displaced persons who are overwhelmed by a culture that is not their own.

Zech seeks to compensate for Langfoot's adversities. In chapter 1, for example, he refers to Langfoot's sporadic correspondence with relatives in Europe who expect him to send them money (something they were accustomed to before, presumably). Furthermore, despite his character's frequent penury and destitution, Zech steadily portrays Langfoot as a proud graduate of Heidelberg University who, rather than describe the true state of his affairs, will pretend in his correspondence home to be on the verge of "another" *Forschungsreise* or scientific expedition, as in chapter 2.

References such as these, plus Langfoot's elaborate interior monologues, his repeated literary allusions, and remarks like those in chapter 15 where Otto Langmann questions Langfoot's need to make his living as a mere peon are, to me, subtle ways of dignifying the protagonist (and author?) in the face of his many tribulations. And by dropping these hints while steadily berating the *indios, criollos,* and *caudillos,* the author seems to imply that under different circumstances, i.e. had he not been in Argentina, his protagonist would have fared much better.

However, the fact of the matter is that Langfoot, like his creator, does not adjust well to the Argentines. Not only do all the natives conspire to brand him a *gringo* simply because he is foreign, but this marginalization also spoils virtually every chance that comes along for him to make a decent living.

It is understandable, therefore, that Langfoot might not be overly fond of the natives. A number of the Argentine women, especially the *indias*, are portrayed in very unflattering terms. However, Langfoot also falls in with some European women of questionable morals, and there are at least as many shiftless Europeans along his way as there are cunning Argentines. Nonetheless, it is the resident Europeans with whom Langfoot prefers to consort and it is the *Einheimische,* or native-born *indios, criollos,* and *caudillos* whom he portrays, with one or two exceptions, as ugly, vulgar, ignorant, and malicious. The ranchers, for example, are inhumane towards the cattle; officials are invariably corrupt; the *caudillos* are likened to Pizarro; invitations by wealthy widows become selfish sexual exploits. This is how the "outsider" (chapter 2, sixth paragraph) lashes back at a culture that won't take him in.

The one important exception to Zech's antipathetic attitude toward the natives consists of a solitary poem incorporated by the author towards the end of chapter 11. It is presented as a song that Langfoot intones at the end of a long day's work. What clearly shines through the lines is a sympathy for the conquered "red men" who fell prey to greedy European invaders in the age of exploration. It is a lament that rings true and parallels many recent (quincentennial) opinions regarding the conquest of the native American peoples. I have to wonder, though, if Zech did not compose it before setting foot in the Americas, or if it was not, as the text says, "someone [else?] had thought [it] up while weeding."

There are also other, quite beautiful ways through which Langfoot finds solace for his Argentine tribulations. Very striking in *The Birds in Langfoot's Belfry*, for example, is the way Zech brings the inanimate to life. Throughout and at regular intervals, he personifies cities, trains, his breast pouch, and even the money inside his breast pouch. Old churches and sawmills, even the Chacarita cemetery, can take on human traits in the author's hands. Abstractions like the cold and the heat, and poverty too, behave like people. But it is especially the manifestations of nature, the sun and the wind in particular, that we sometimes see parade across the pampas in regal splendor, and at other times find quietly curled up in the woods. Beautiful fantasies such as these are substituted for the human warmth found wanting in exile.

The nature passages were also the ones I enjoyed translating the most. I suppose this is because I come closest to being an "impressionist" translator who trusts her heart first and her dictionary second. For me what counts most is the ability to empathize, along with a command of the source and target languages and familiarity with the author and his period. For this reason I was happy to see *The Birds in Langfoot's Belfry* conclude with a "homecoming" for Langfoot. His new *home* is among friendly Europeans, it is true, yet he has adapted enough to resolve his old malaise. By accepting hospitality and employment from the Langmanns, Langfoot's struggle against the odds has come to an end. But after all is said and done, he and the Langmanns, like their creator, remain securely in Argentina.

Elena B. Odio
March 1994